THE TRUTH ABOUT SUPERVISION

ABOUT THE AUTHOR

Anne O'Brien Carelli, Ph.D., is the owner of Carelli & Associates, a management training and consulting business in Delmar, New York. Her clients have included corporations such as KeyCorp, McDonald's, General Electric, and Parke-Davis, and numerous health care and educational organizations, government agencies, manufacturing plants, and small businesses. She has assisted organizations in restructuring to team-based management, establishing performance appraisal, job interviewing, and customer service systems, and implementing rewards and recognition programs. She is a public speaker, college instructor, and author of a number of client business publications. She is the former Director of the New York State Equity Center and Executive Director of the New York State Association for Women in Administration.

THE TRUTH ABOUT SUPERVISION

Coaching, Teamwork, Interviewing, Appraisals, 360° Assessments, and Recognition

By

ANNE O'BRIEN CARELLI, PH.D.

CHARLES C THOMAS • PUBLISHER, LTD.
Springfield • Illinois • U.S.A.

Published and Distributed Throughout the World by

CHARLES C THOMAS • PUBLISHER, LTD.
2600 South First Street
Springfield, Illinois 62704

©2004 by CHARLES C THOMAS • PUBLISHER, LTD.

ISBN 0-398-07470-4 (hard)
ISBN 0-398-07471-2(paper)

Library of Congress Catalog Card Number: 2003061379

With THOMAS BOOKS *careful attention is given to all details of manufacturing and design. It is the Publisher's desire to present books that are satisfactory as to their physical qualities and artistic possibilities and appropriate for their particular use.* THOMAS BOOKS *will be true to those laws of quality that assure a good name and good will.*

Printed in the United States of America
CR-R-3

Library of Congress Cataloging-in-Publication Data

Carelli, Anne O'Brien.
   The truth about supervision : coaching, teamwork, interviewing,
appraisals, 3600 assessments, and recognition / Anne O'Brien
Carelli.
      p. cm.
   Includes index.
   ISBN 0-398-07470-4 -- ISBN 0-398-07471-2 (pbk.)
   1. Supervision of employees--Handbook, manuals, etc. 2.
Leadership--Handbooks, manuals, etc. 3. Employee motivation--
Handbooks, manuals, etc. I. Title.

HF5549.12.C3555 2004
658.3'02--dc22

                                                                  2003061379

PREFACE

Maria heaved a big sigh as she flipped through her calendar. As supervisor of a large department, she was used to days that were jam-packed with multiple responsibilities. She was, however, starting to feel overwhelmed.

She knew that there would always be the routine supervisory tasks that required her attention, such as keeping track of budgets and time and attendance, monitoring safety and efficiency goals for the department, and responding to employee concerns.

She knew that there would be larger projects that demanded her leadership, such as the reorganization of her department, customer service training, and the implementation of a new software system.

She had only been the supervisor for eight months, but was adjusting to the constant interruptions, problems to solve, and new assignments.

But just when she was beginning to understand the responsibilities of a supervisor, Maria was reminded by her manager that her employee performance appraisals were way overdue, and she was late in selecting an employee to receive a service award. In addition, she was supposed to conduct interviews for a new accountant, and she needed to write a plan for teambuilding.

Although Maria had a general idea about how to implement these tasks, she needed specific information on what was really involved in carrying them out effectively. She wanted clear-cut steps, down-to-earth advice, and practical recommendations.

This book is for supervisors like Maria who need realistic information about how to do some of the principal tasks of a supervisor. It provides detailed information for both new and experienced supervisors, as well as for employees and students who desire to become supervisors.

This book was created in response to thousands of participants in supervisory training programs who were seeking basic, frank information about how to conduct key tasks of a supervisor. The training participants were busy carrying out the same tasks as Maria, often making significant decisions based on fast consultation with colleagues, quick perusals of literature, and just plain gut instinct. They repeatedly indicated in training sessions that they needed a resource that would quickly supply them with succinct answers to questions about supervisory issues. The training participants indicated that the responsibilities requiring specific guidance were:

- guiding and *coaching* for employee development rather than discipline
- conducting job *interviews* that are informative and fair
- designing and implementing *teamwork*
- carrying out comfortable and effective *performance appraisals*, including *360° Assessments* that involve multiple evaluations
- *delegating* important tasks so that supervisors can release work to employees who willingly accept the challenge
- *recognizing* employees for their accomplishments and *rewarding* them for making positive contributions.

The Truth About Supervision: Coaching, Teamwork, Interviewing, Appraisals, 360° Assessments, and Recognition was designed for supervisors who work in factories, hospitals, banks, offices, or any other work setting, because the essential tasks of a supervisor are universally similar. The chapters are written in a question-and-answer format that allows supervisors to research a specific problem or read an overview of a topic.

Many of the questions addressed were raised repeatedly in classes for new supervisors, as well as in training sessions with experienced supervisors. The examples of true experiences that are included in the book are from a variety of workplaces such as manufacturing plants, health care centers, educational organizations, and businesses.

The material contained in this book is based on the author's experiences and observations of good practices. Supervisors should discuss the contents of the chapters with colleagues and managers. Whenever supervisors implement a new activity or program, especially in an effort to comply with any law, they should consult with their Human Resources/Personnel department and/or obtain the advice of a legal representative of the organization.

ACKNOWLEDGMENTS

This book evolved from years of consulting with supervisors who were brave enough to share their concerns, ideas, and frustrations in professional training programs. They had to admit that they did not always know how to do their jobs effectively, and they participated in the training sessions with open minds and a willingness to self-assess and learn. My thanks to the thousands of training participants who asked questions, shared stories, and tackled problems. As all teachers know, you learn something new every day from your students.

Thank you to Wendy Millheiser Barnett and Barbara Kelly for assisting in the preparation of the text.

Thank you, of course, to Frank, Caitlin, and John, who understand that I could never write a book about managing a kitchen, and thank you to Ellen Saunders, Kathy O'Brien, Debbie Vertanin, Linda Scatton, Suzanne Brownrigg, Cindy Aleksa Mason, and Jennifer Dodge Johnson for your vital support.

Special thanks goes to the employees of Blue Circle Cement in Ravena, New York. At that plant (and up in the quarry) you will find hard-working, dedicated, good-humored problem-solvers who are not always easily supervised, but a constant source of valuable information and insight.

CONTENTS

THE TRUTH ABOUT SUPERVISION

Chapter 1

THE TRUTH ABOUT COACHING

I guess I better reserve an hour for coaching.
(Customer Service Supervisor, preparing to discipline an employee.)

Coaching is not disciplining and it should never take an hour. When a supervisor stops an employee in the hall and quickly reviews a new procedure, that is *coaching*. When the supervisor meets privately for a few minutes with an employee and provides ideas about how to improve a presentation, that is *coaching*. When the supervisor calls an employee into the office and *briefly* reviews expectations about work policies, that is *coaching*.

Coaching allows supervisors the opportunity to provide employees with information, support, and direction. Supervisors who understand the purpose of coaching discover that it is a valuable managerial tool.

Supervisors who are good coaches realize that coaching is a short interaction with one employee who needs immediate guidance. It is not a review of performance in general, or a disciplinary session. It is not meant for identifying employees who are failing at their jobs, or for warning employees who refuse to meet organizational standards. Coaching is an educational process, designed for steering employees in the right direction, and for providing information and support so that employees can succeed.

Coaching is based on the premise that employees want to learn and want to do things correctly. Coaching allows supervisors to intervene when they spot confused or struggling employees, or employees who are not following organizational policies or procedures. By coaching, supervisors can guide employees back on track. If the coaching is done in an efficient and sensitive manner, then employees learn from the experience and welcome the interest and guidance of their supervisors.

This chapter covers the purpose of coaching, as well as the steps and strategies that can assist supervisors in coaching effectively.

3

1. WHAT EXACTLY IS COACHING?

The term *coaching* conjures up images of an athletic coach, whistle in hand, yelling from the sidelines and lecturing in the locker room. Coaching in the workplace is not quite as dramatic. Effective supervisors are actually coaching their employees throughout the entire workday because most coaching is informal, and takes place "on the run," requiring a few minutes of quick, focused interaction.

Coaching does not mean long conversations, tension-filled dialogues, and written goals and action plans. It does not mean that an employee is in "big trouble" and needs to be put back in line. It does not mean that discipline is necessary, and a closed-door meeting is in order. Coaching occurs when a supervisor observes a behavior that indicates that an employee needs quick guidance. Before the employee can get completely off track, the supervisor connects with the employee, provides information and encouragement, and then moves on. Coaching takes place when it is necessary to prevent a minor problem from getting worse.

The employee gains new knowledge and direction from coaching, as well as support from the supervisor. Coaching can take two minutes or 15 minutes, but it rarely becomes a lengthy conversation unless additional problems surface.

Supervisors know that they are coaching when the interaction with the employee is an *intervention* that is *individualized* and *instructional.*

It is a quick *intervention* when a supervisor spots the *first signs* of:

- faulty work behavior
- lagging work behavior
- employee confusion, complaining, or work avoidance
- employee unrealistic expectations
- employee need for encouragement.

The coaching session is *individualized* because it is conducted privately, one-to-one, and immediately after the need for intervention is determined.

The coaching is *instructional* because the purpose of the coaching session is to quickly educate employees. For example, employees may need to be reminded about expectations, deadlines, and standards.

They may not have realized that they are failing to follow organizational policies or procedures. They may be falling behind because they need help with time management or skill development. It is the responsibility of supervisors to catch the first signs of stumbling, and then to coach employees so that they can learn how to improve. The employees will then feel confident that supervisors will provide support and guidance.

Once supervisors understand that a major part of their job is to educate employees, then coaching happens automatically. It means that supervisors are teaching when it is needed, keeping an eye out for employees who may need assistance, and praising when improvements occur.

2. WHY IS IT IMPORTANT TO COACH?

Coaching is essential because it is better to catch a problem in its initial stages than to wait until employees are really in trouble. Since coaching is a quick, informal intervention, the results can be an immediate change in the behavior of employees.

Although it is often tempting to ignore a problem to see if the employee solves it, or to avoid an interaction with an employee because it might be tense, it is better to step in, provide guidance, and then step back again. The employee now knows what the supervisor expects, and, if appropriate information is provided, the employee can concentrate on getting work done effectively.

Coaching also tells employees that the supervisor is paying close attention, has expertise and ideas to share, and is interested in assisting employees in doing their best work. If coaching is done on a routine basis, then employees are not threatened by the process. They see it as an opportunity to learn how they are doing and to gain clear direction on what they can do better.

Although coaching is not intended to serve as a substitute for performance appraisals, the coaching session can provide valuable information that can contribute to annual appraisals. For example, if a supervisor notices that Mary Jane is frequently coming to meetings unprepared, a quick coaching session can raise the concern, get to the root of the problem, clarify expectations, and get Mary Jane back on track. The supervisor has fulfilled the important role of educator and guide. Mary Jane knows what needs to be corrected. When it is time for the performance appraisal, Mary Jane is not suddenly blindsided by the supervisor's concerns. In fact, the performance appraisal may show that Mary Jane is always well prepared for meetings. The coaching session provided her with important direction so that her overall appraisal reflects her accomplishments, rather than problems that could have been solved with timely coaching.

3. WHEN SHOULD SUPERVISORS COACH?

Coaching should only be carried out privately, and as soon after the precipitating event as possible. Supervisors should avoid causing stress for the employee by loudly announcing the need to meet, or by leaving "SEE ME" notes. Coaching will not go well if the employee approaches the session with trepidation. "I need to see you in my office—NOW" does not imply that an informal, relaxed coaching session is about to take place.

Coaching should take place when the issue at hand can be discussed in five to 15 minutes, and no longer. If the topic requires a more elaborate, intense conversation, then the term *coaching* can no longer be applied. Specific examples of coaching topics are:

- explaining protocol or policies that may be confusing
- suggesting tips for improving interpersonal relations
- providing ideas for motivating coworkers
- assisting in organizing priorities
- identifying errors and explaining how to correct them
- reassuring when projects are moving slowly
- suggesting faster ways of completing tasks
- providing contacts and connections to facilitate tasks
- explaining goals and objectives to encourage focus
- clarifying the reasons for a task
- expressing concern and ideas related to quality or safety
- orienting a new employee to something new
- reminding an experienced employee about standards
- demonstrating how to complete a task

• encouraging perseverance
• informing about training and steps to advancement.

In most cases, especially if the supervisor coaches well, the coaching session will be well received, and the employee will understand how to improve behavior.

4. HOW IS COACHING DIFFERENT FROM DISCIPLINE?

There may seem to be a fine line between coaching and disciplining employees, but once a supervisor incorporates coaching into daily routines, it becomes easier to understand the difference. Coaching is meant to alert employees to something that needs correcting. It focuses on concrete steps to improvement. If the coaching is successful, behavior changes are evident right away.

For example, suppose Fred wandered into the office on time but socialized for 15 minutes before settling down to work. Originally, he did this once or twice a week and the supervisor was not very concerned. Fred was a good worker and did not seem to waste time during the rest of the day. His colleagues were also conscientious about their work. In this work setting, there was some flexibility in how work was completed. However, when Fred started to make a daily habit of socializing and was beginning to get others involved in a similar habit, the supervisor did a quick coaching session. The session was informal and informative, with expectations presented clearly. Fred and his supervisor discussed the advantages of a flexible workplace, but the necessary limits to socializing. Fred agreed to curtail his morning socializing and the behavior changed the next morning.

The supervisor may have to gently remind Fred once or twice, or may have to send a subtle signal to Fred so that he can stay on track. The supervisor may also have to quietly coach other employees, explaining the reasons for curtailing the morning social hour. But coaching alone should fix the problem.

However, if Fred makes promises and does not keep them, or if Fred refuses to cooperate, then the supervisor has moved out of the coaching domain. It is now necessary to be more firm about the consequences of Fred's behavior. Fred may need to understand that he is no longer being reminded about what is expected of him so that he can change the behavior, but that he has now entered the first steps of discipline with more significant consequences. Depending upon the organizational policy, it may require that the supervisor give a verbal warning, write a formal disciplinary memorandum, or clearly articulate possible actions such as transfers, task changes, or review of assignments and hours.

Supervisors often struggle with how many reminders it must take before coaching switches to discipline. This is especially true when the problems are related to "time and attendance." If the supervisor has stepped in at the first sign of a problem (or pattern of a problem), has discussed expectations and solutions, and has obtained employee commitment to new behaviors, the coaching is complete. For some employees, it may take a repeat of the coaching session, reiterating the key points and stressing that the next session will focus on discipline. If the employee has been warned that discipline is next and the behavior still does not change, then it is time to begin the formal discipline process.

5. HOW IS COACHING DIFFERENT FROM COUNSELING?

Although the terms are sometimes used interchangeably, coaching is not counseling. *Coaching* is when supervisors quickly intervene to provide direction to an employee when a work-related problem arises. *Counseling* is provided by the supervisor or by other sources when an employee has personal problems that are not work-related. Supervisors should not be "counseling" employees unless the supervisor has specific training in mental health counseling and/or has been given the responsibility and authority for employee counseling.

The employee's personal problems, such as a pending divorce, a sick child, financial concerns, and so forth, may be influencing work behaviors because the employee is stressed, distracted, and perhaps emotional during the workday. The employee may be making personal phone calls, venting frustrations with coworkers, and struggling with productivity and attendance.

Supervisors can *coach* employees who are struggling with personal problems by doing the following:

1. Express concerns about the employee's well-being, but do not gather personal details or reveal knowledge of details. (In some cases, the supervisor may only be guessing that something is wrong.) If the employee appears to be using the time to confide in the supervisor, then listen only. Of course, the type of relationship between the supervisor and the employee may determine the degree of sympathy and support. The supervisor should keep in mind that relationships can be strained when a supervisor wants to support an employee because they are friends, but wants to maintain professional interaction as well. Listening without expressing a personal point of view may be best if the employee feels comfortable revealing details. (Note: if the details are too uncomfortable for the supervisor, or if they are alarming, or suggest possible legal problems, go immediately to step 4 below, and then return to steps 2 and 3.)

2. Provide specific information about policies and expectations at work, reminding the employee that everyone is expected to comply. Indicate that the employee does not need the added problem of a job in jeopardy.

3. If possible, discuss possible accommodations for the employee, such as flexible work hours, access to a phone, changes in assignments, and so forth. Stress the short-term nature of the adjustments and the limits to the accommodations. Recognize that other employees may not understand the changes, especially if they do not know about the employee's situation. Make sure the accommodations are short-term.

4. Encourage the employee to seek professional help, stressing the value of talking to experts about a problem. (Consult with Human Resources/Personnel about whether the counseling can be required.) Provide specific information about counseling resources such as Employee Assistance Programs, credit counseling services, clinical facilities, law enforcement, or legal services. Make sure that the services are preapproved by the organization. It may be necessary for the supervisor to hand the employee a list of suggested counseling resources (or a few business cards) so that the employee can decide the most appropriate resource to call. If the employee's problems appear to be especially serious (or they are profoundly affecting work behaviors) the supervisor should consult Human Resources/Personnel to determine the best means of providing an employee with guidance, while maintaining standards and productivity at work.

6. HOW IS COACHING DIFFERENT FROM PERFORMANCE APPRAISALS?

Coaching is a quick, informal, instructional session that is initiated by the supervisor when a problem becomes evident. It is intended to call attention to a concern and provide immediate employee guidance. A coaching session occurs when an employee is faltering, needs motivation, or requires clear direction. Coaching is about one specific work-related behavior. If coaching is conducted effectively, then supervisors will observe an immediate change in the employee's behavior.

Performance appraisals take place on a regular basis (usually annually) and are a summary of accomplishments and goals. Performance appraisals cover a variety of behaviors and work activities, and are usually designed to give employees a general assessment of their work, as well as a plan for the future.

If a performance appraisal is conducted effectively, then past coaching topics are not even mentioned unless the results of the coaching are worth noting in the appraisal paperwork (e.g., obvious long-term changes in behavior, completed projects, improved productivity). It is inevitable that the discussion of the employee's overall performance will include guidance and direction as needed, but no employee should ever be blindsided at an appraisal meeting about a specific problem that should have been addressed earlier.

7. WHAT SHOULD A SUPERVISOR DO BEFORE COACHING?

Before stepping in to conduct a coaching session, the supervisor should do a quick mental checklist of the following questions:

- What exactly does the employee need to know?
- Has the employee already been informed about what is expected?
- Does the employee have the necessary resources, including equipment, support staff, and *time*?
- Does the supervisor model what is expected?
- Is the employee being singled out when the problem actually involves others as well?

- Does the employee have the necessary skills, training, or experiential background?
- Is there something the supervisor could have done to prevent the problem?

If the supervisor runs through this list of questions, it may become obvious that the employee had no choice but to falter. For example, if the proper tools were not provided, or the standard operating procedures were not explained, or the deadlines were unrealistic, then the supervisor needs to recognize that the employee may not be at fault. If the supervisor looks in the mirror before the coaching session and asks, "Is there something that I could have done to assist this employee sooner?" the session will be far more effective.

Once the supervisor has determined what the employee needs and how to best meet the needs, the coaching session can begin. Occasionally, the supervisor will be surprised by employee questions and concerns that were unexpected. This is all the more reason to get the coaching session going, and to open up communication. The employee gets assistance on getting back on track, and the supervisor learns about how to be more supportive.

---

8. WHAT SHOULD BE INCLUDED IN A COACHING SESSION?

The approach to the coaching session can often determine the outcome. After the supervisor has contemplated the purpose of the coaching, then the following steps should take place, keeping in mind that most coaching does not take longer than 15 minutes:

1. Invite the employee to talk.

Using a relaxed, nonthreatening tone of voice (and watch the body language!), indicate that there is a concern that needs to be discussed. Set the tone by being serious but friendly, beginning the statement with "I."

- I'm confused about something. . .
- I'm getting concerned. . .

- I think I'd better help you with something . . .
- I've noticed. . .

2. Get to the point right away.

Explain the concern so that the employee does not have time to get nervous or defensive. Again, try to avoid the word *you*. (This is hard to do!) Be very specific so that the employee knows exactly what the meeting is about:

- The deadline was last week.
- The error rate is up.
- The material I needed was not presented.
- The project does not seem to be progressing.

3. Immediately indicate faith that the problem can be corrected, setting a tone of support, rather than discipline:

- I think we can get to the bottom of this.
- I'm sure we can straighten this out.
- Let's figure this out.
- This is unusual for you.

4. Do not go any further until the employee agrees that there is a problem, even if the specifics still need to be discussed. The best way to do this is by asking a question:

- Do you agree?
- Can you fill me in?
- What's going on?
- Is this something you have been concerned about?

The employee's response will reveal either *confusion, denial,* or *agreement.* For confusion and denial, it may be necessary for the supervisor to restate observations and concerns, and to ask the employee if the observations are on target. Ask the employee to elaborate so that a complete picture (two perspectives) of the problem can be obtained. This can move the employee from defensiveness to explanations.

There may be long detailed background information, or even excuses, but employees can provide valuable information as they respond. Solutions to the problem can only be discussed if the employee agrees that a problem exists.

Stress that the goal is to get back on track and get back to work. (If the employee continues to insist that there is no problem and indicates that the supervisor's observations are incorrect, provide plenty of opportunities for the employee to explain. If the employee refuses, go to step 6 below.)

5. Discuss what is expected and determine if the expectations can be met. This is the time to talk about resources, policies, and procedures with both the supervisor and employee providing suggestions for improving the situation. This is when the supervisor can facilitate a change in employee behavior by reviewing a deadline, teaching a methodology, helping with priorities, making a phone call to a crucial contact, setting up training, reviewing an employee handbook excerpt, and so forth.

The supervisor should make sure that:

- expectations have been made very clear
- information and education have taken place
- ideas about solutions have been discussed
- the employee has participated in the problem-solving, sharing concerns and ideas
- decisions about future behavior have been agreed upon.

6. It may be necessary to articulate consequences if there is an indication that the problem behavior may not be corrected. The coaching session can usually end after step 5 when solutions are discussed and the employee has a better understanding of what to do next. But, occasionally, it is necessary to reinforce the expectations by pointing out the consequences if behaviors do not change. In other words, sometimes the supervisor has to be a little more emphatic. The consequences can be *natural*, occurring automatically, or they can be *imposed* by the supervisor. The employee may need to hear what the consequences could be, but only if there is a sense of resistance or lack of employee commitment. Examples are:

Natural Consequences

"Your coworkers will not be able to complete their work until your part is done, resulting in longer hours."
"The budget will be late if the figures are incorrect, impacting expenses in our department."

Imposed Consequences

"I will have to move to a disciplinary process, which we both want to avoid, if we can help it."
"I will have to consult with the manager of the department to determine what we need to do next about your role in this problem."

In most coaching sessions the consequences are readily apparent, and the employee does not need to be reminded. This step is only necessary if the supervisor does not feel completely confident that the coaching messages were well received.

7. Repeat the solutions.

Just to make sure, the supervisor should reiterate what has been agreed upon during the coaching session. Then the supervisor can feel confident that both parties understood the solution, and follow-up actions are clear.

8. End the session with a thank-you, a compliment, and an offer to provide further assistance:

I knew I could count on you.
You are always willing to work hard.
I appreciate your attitude about solving this problem.
Let me know if you need assistance later on.

Be careful not to be patronizing, but clearly pleased with the results of the conversation. Following the steps above can facilitate a smooth and speedy coaching session. If coaching is routine, then employees will become familiar with the format and will eventually turn to the supervisor for coaching.

9. WHAT IF THE COACHING SESSION IS NOT WORKING?

If the supervisor has attempted to follow the steps to coaching but is still met with confusion or resistance, then some of the following factors may be involved:

- the tone of the supervisor is negative and aggressive
- trust and respect between the parties is minimal
- the supervisor has a history of lecturing and disciplining, rather than guiding and supporting
- the employee has a history of pretending to agree and then ignoring the agreements
- the employee would rather explain than listen
- the supervisor is providing too much information without being specific
- the expectations are unrealistic
- other employees make achievement difficult
- the employee may have the enthusiasm but not the capability to complete a task
- the problem has actually reached a disciplinary stage.

Then there are always factors such as politics, budgets, morale, competition, job security, union friction, and many other issues that can influence the success of the coaching session. Coaching can go awry for a myriad of reasons, but an alert supervisor can be prepared for possible obstacles to a successful session.

Supervisors can overcome a number of negative variables if they open the coaching session with a positive, helpful tone, making it clear that a minor problem needs to be fixed before it becomes a major issue. This sends the immediate message that the employee is not being questioned or disciplined, but assisted by the supervisor. Supervisors may have to wait it out as the employee (especially one who does not trust the supervisor, feels insecure in the job, or is barely an average worker) feels compelled to tell another side of the story. As the employee talks, details can come out that provide clarification. Supervisors can turn around a floundering coaching session if they listen, do not argue, provide praise and optimism, and involve the employee in solving the problem. Useful, open-ended questions are:

What do you think is *really* causing the problem?
What do you think we should do about this?
Is there anything I can do to assist you?
What can speed this along?
What would help to eliminate the confusion/frustration/annoyance?

The answers to these questions may be revealing. The solutions that are recommended by the employee may be impossible to achieve, but at least the supervisor has a better sense of the emotions and the thoughts of the employee. The goal is to determine, *together*, what *is* possible, while reinforcing expectations and supporting the employee. If the session begins to get too emotional, then the supervisor should suggest meeting again later when everyone is calm. If a later session is still not working, either defer to another manager or move to discipline.

If employees feel that the coaching conversation is an actual dialogue and not a lecture or a reprimand, then agreement on solutions will occur more easily. If the supervisor maintains a consistent daily pattern of supportive coaching and follows through on promises, then each session will get a little bit easier.

10. WHAT ARE COACHING PHRASES THAT SHOULD NEVER BE USED?

The following phrases have actually been used to open coaching sessions, instantly creating a negative tone and raising anxiety and resistance:

I need to see you later.
We have a problem.
What in the world are you doing?
I heard something that concerns me.
Someone told me. . .
Those are just excuses.
I don't believe that. . .
That can't be true. . .
You didn't. . .

You were seen. . .
Let me give you some advice. . .
Here's what you need to know. . .
You don't get it. . .
I question your judgment/values/perspective. . .
You should have. . .
I've taken notes on your behavior. . .
I'm surprised that someone with your background/of your
    gender/with your social life/of your age and experience, etc. . . . .

The list can easily continue with many other examples of phrases that can immediately change the tone of the coaching session. Supervisors who want to coach successfully need to put themselves in the shoes of the recipient of the coaching. How does it feel to be coached? How can it feel comfortable, informative, and helpful? Is it unbiased and fair? Do both parties participate?

The coaching session can be informative and positive if the supervisor refrains from being accusatory or patronizing, encourages input from the employee, willingly acknowledges the need for more supervisory assistance, and sets a friendly, professional tone. The best supervisors are able to accomplish this even when the employee is especially difficult to supervise.

11. WHAT ARE THE CHARACTERISTICS OF AN EXCELLENT COACH?

For some supervisors, coaching is easy and automatic. They have been able to establish routine, informal discussions with employees when guidance seems to be necessary. They have a style that facilitates open communication, and have developed trust and respect so that employees welcome coaching.

But even comfortable coaches can find that the process of coaching takes hard work, skill, and perseverance. The skills can be developed, and with every session, coaching will improve. The hard work and perseverance means that supervisors have to be willing to take time out of *every day* to quickly coach one or more employees. It means that difficult employees still need to be approached and difficult topics still need to be addressed.

If supervisors recognize that coaching is a significant part of being a leader, and if they believe that short coaching sessions can ultimately save a lot of time, then it is easier to develop the necessary characteristics to coach successfully.

Excellent coaches are:

- able to establish employee trust because they listen, take employee concerns seriously, share knowledge, and follow through on promises
- calm and patient even during times that are tense
- willing to listen, even when an employee seems to want to justify unsatisfactory behavior—recognizing that good listeners learn more about their employees
- able to describe concerns clearly, honing in on the root of a problem
- able to focus on solutions, direction, and valuable information for the employee
- able to provide expertise, contacts, resources, training, and time, so that employees can develop skills and connections
- very specific about expectations and standards, without assuming that the employee can read the supervisor's mind
- willing to consider the style, interests, expertise, and motivation of the employee being coached
- able to maintain confidentiality if possible
- are encouraging, positive, and supportive.

Supervisors know that they have become excellent coaches when they and their employees do not even realize that a coaching "session" has occurred because the coaching process has become a welcome routine.

Chapter 2

THE TRUTH ABOUT TEAMWORK

I want you all to work in teams from now on.
(Nurse Manager, speaking to hospital nurses attending an annual
planning meeting.)

It is easy to tell when an organization has established a successful team-based management system. Employees routinely take the initiative to meet together to discuss how to achieve the goals of the day and the mission of the organization. They analyze their responsibilities and progress, and make recommendations about productivity, safety, and cost-effective policies and procedures. Supervisors work closely with their teams to determine what needs to be accomplished, and then leave it up to the teams to decide how to get it done. They provide consultation and direction but are free to work on managerial tasks while the teams concentrate on organizing the workday. In a strong team-based environment, there is constant open communication, trust, and a routine flow of ideas and problem-solving.

Is this really possible? Can groups of people work together so well that they share in decision-making, openly express opinions, and determine priorities and job assignments? Can employees really feel as if their ideas and suggestions are taken seriously? Can supervisors feel comfortable empowering employees to take on tasks that were traditionally the responsibility of management?

It is possible. True teamwork exists in a variety of organizations, including large processing plants, international financial institutions, nonprofit organizations, and small businesses. Team-based management is based on the notion that employees at all levels bring unique skills, creativity, and experience to their jobs, and those qualities should be recognized and cultivated. If the talents of all employees are tapped, then the organization benefits with more ideas and better decisions. Many organizations have discovered that quality teamwork results in improvements in all aspects of the workplace.

In organizations that have a true commitment to maintaining teamwork, with the concerns of both managers and employees taken into consideration, it is possible to establish a team-based climate that is comfortable and productive.

Supervisors are crucial in the team-building process. Their understanding of the purpose and benefits of teams, as well as the phases of implementation, play an important role in establishing a team-based environment that is supported by all levels of the organization. In this chapter, key elements of team-building are discussed, including the phases of teamwork, the steps to implementing teams, the role of leadership, and strategies for overcoming barriers to establishing successful team-based management.

1. WHAT EXACTLY IS A "TEAM"?

A "team" in the workplace is different than a traditional "work group" because of the high level of employee interaction and communication. The emphasis is on sharing information, gathering ideas, and coming to agreement on the best ways to get jobs done. "Teamwork" in any type of organization, whether it is an office, manufacturing plant, or hospital, means that employees:

- set and monitor work goals together
- establish systems of team communication
- routinely meet to share information
- work closely with supervisors to plan and carry out work
- routinely participate in decisions that affect daily work
- routinely provide input into organizational decisions
- make daily decisions without supervisory approval
- evaluate the effectiveness of communication
- have many opportunities to share expertise and to develop skills and interests.

In many cases, teams are expected to make decisions related to their daily work, without supervisory direction. The teams meet often, determine work assignments of team members, and monitor everyone's progress. The teams constantly check to see how they are doing in achieving goals that they have defined as a team.

Teams in the workplace can be organized in many different configurations. Some organizations break employees into teams that have a mixture of specializations, stressing the value of diverse perspectives. Other organizations establish teams for special projects or short-term assignments, while others create teams by units, professions, or work areas.

For example, the maintenance department of a processing plant may be expected to operate as a team. They set team goals, determine work flow and job assignments, and meet regularly to evaluate procedures and progress and to make decisions.

In another example, a team of engineers may be established to work on a capital project. They may have different areas of expertise but are expected to pool their knowledge and resources and plan the project together. They determine as a team how they will monitor progress, and work as a team to solve problems, with minimal managerial oversight.

In a third example, a corporation safety team or quality control team may be pulled together to represent various levels and departments. The entire team is responsible for overseeing consistency in organizational policies and procedures. They establish protocols that make sense throughout the organization, and keep each other informed about new data, upcoming problems, and creative solutions. Because they are a "team" and not a "committee," they are expected to maintain constant communication, share knowledge, work for the betterment of the organization (reduce turf wars, streamline process), establish goals that the entire plant can meet successfully, and come to agreement about the best way to achieve the goals.

In all of these examples, there is direction from the organizational leadership, but the team has the freedom to organize their work so that they can use their brainpower and experience to achieve goals. Some organizations cultivate a *climate* of teamwork, emphasizing that employees are expected to meet often and share knowledge, even if they are not formally structured into teams.

In a team-based environment, regardless of the type of structure, employees on teams are expected to:

- share what they know
- apply their expertise and build the skills of team members
- tap the talents of coworkers
- communicate on a regular basis, even if it means critiquing the way things are done
- gather different ideas so that problems can be solved more effectively
- resolve conflicts to save time and money, and to improve safety, productivity, and relationships
- make decisions about daily work, rather than rely on supervisor direction and approval.

2. WHAT IS THE PURPOSE OF TEAMS?

Team-based organizations recognize that employees have knowledge, suggestions, experience, and creative ideas to contribute. The primary purpose of teams is to utilize the brainpower of employees because their expertise is valued.

Diverse perspectives from team members can provide new insights and better solutions to problems. In a work climate that supports teams, finding solutions to daily problems is not limited to management. It is assumed that workers on the front line may have valuable observations that can shed new light on a problem. It is taken for granted that multiple perspectives lead to the best decisions.

When employees are asked for ideas and opinions and are involved in making decisions about their daily work, they are not only better informed, they are more committed to getting work done effectively. If they work together to make a decision, they are more invested in making sure that the results are successful.

This is not to say that teams should be making all decisions without benefit of supervision. In the most effective teamwork, supervisors and teams routinely make decisions together. The supervisor provides information about organizational goals and expectations, and then works with the team to get their perspective on the best way to achieve the goals and get the work done.

3. WHAT DO TEAMS LOOK LIKE?

Teams usually consist of four to ten employees, often including a supervisor or team leader as members of the team. The team must be able to communicate on a regular basis, either by meeting together at the work site, connecting electronically (virtual teams), or conferring by teleconference.

Examples of teams might be:

• A shipping department is expected to work as a team so that forklift operators, packers, dispatchers, and other employees in the department create an efficient shipping operation. They become familiar with each other's tasks and problems, and may even cross-train. They brainstorm improvements and set goals together. They eliminate duplication of effort and build communication, helping each other out when necessary. They meet at the beginning of a shift to communicate with the previous shift and to plan the work schedule. They do not depend on a supervisor to direct their work, but plan and implement together *with* the supervisor, using their experiential background and creative thinking.

• A nursing home establishes patient-focused teams. Twice a day a team of caretakers (doctors, aides, rehabilitation specialists, nurses, nutritionists, etc.) meets to compare observations about residents. Different perspectives come together to provide better patient care. The doctors may have the final say on treatment, but representatives from many areas of specialization are pooled together for better decision-making.

• A manufacturing company creates teams for different projects. Team members are selected on the basis of their expertise and possible contribution to the project. Representatives from the accounting, environmental, or parts departments may be included on the team to provide a company-wide perspective. The team members are expected to take advantage of the collection of knowledge on the team, communicate so that work progresses smoothly, and regularly put their heads together to plan work and to solve problems. Team members may be located somewhere other than the project site, but they "meet" regularly via e-mail, phone, and teleconferencing.

It is easy to tell if an organization is truly committed to teams if the following behaviors are in evidence:

- Supervisors consult with teams on many daily decisions.
- Goals are posted and monitored by workers (not only by management).
- Teams meet, formally and informally, with team members consulting with each other and with other teams.
- Team members determine priorities, work distribution, and procedures, in consultation with management.
- Team member ideas, expertise, and suggestions are seriously considered when supervisors/managers are making decisions.

Teamwork is desirable for many reasons, such as:

- Employees are given opportunities to provide knowledge and suggestions, resulting in better procedures and products.
- Employees are more satisfied because they have been asked for their ideas and opinions, resulting in better work habits and stronger loyalty.
- Supervisors are able to make better decisions because they are constantly gathering ideas and information from their teams.
- Supervisors have better relationships with employees, significantly reducing the traditional "us versus them" mentality.
- Supervisors can release some of their responsibilities to teams, reducing their own workload and empowering employees.

These statements are true, of course, if teamwork is implemented and maintained properly. Leaders of the organization must be truly committed to inviting employee participation in decision-making. Guidelines for team involvement in decision-making must be established, and team members must be truly invested in sharing knowledge so that procedures can be the best practices.

5. WHAT MAKES AN EXCELLENT TEAM-BASED ORGANIZATION?

The keys to establishing and maintaining excellent teamwork are:

- Senior management is committed to employee involvement in decision-making.
- A committee, team, or point person is responsible for maintaining effective teamwork.
- A design and time frame for rolling out teamwork has been created with employee involvement.
- Teams are organized in a manner that facilitates communication and productivity.
- Teams, including all management, are trained in team-building, including communication and conflict resolution skills, decision-making strategies, benchmarking, and systems for tracking progress.
- Teams are well informed about the organization's vision, mission, goals, and changes.
- Guidelines for decision-making are clearly established.
- Teams, with supervisory guidance, set long-term and short-term goals.
- Teams take responsibility for working well as a team.
- Teams demonstrate accountability for their decisions. (If supervisors work with teams to make decisions, accountability is clear and less blaming occurs.)
- Teams determine steps to achieve goals, solve problems, resolve differences, and monitor progress.
- Teams meet routinely to determine distribution of work, priorities, changes in procedures and priorities, and other daily work challenges.
- Management routinely consults with team members to gather their input, explaining the role of the team in making final decisions.
- Management takes ideas seriously, not asking and ignoring, or, worse yet, deciding before asking.
- Team members understand the difference between "input" and "final decision."
- The organization supports teamwork by authorizing training, visits to other team-based organizations, and recognition of team accomplishments.

6. WHAT DO EMPLOYEES GAIN FROM TEAMS?

Employees who work in successful team-based organizations gain:

- a sense of accomplishment for setting and achieving goals that make sense to them
- self-respect for making regular contributions to organizational decisions
- growth in knowledge as they learn from their fellow team members
- opportunities to apply skills and try new ideas
- a better sense of their personal contribution to the organization (especially in large corporations)
- security in feeling informed about organizational plans and changes
- recognition for achievements, creative problem-solving, and support of fellow team members
- opportunities for advancement as they are able to share suggestions and ideas, and to reveal skills and interests
- appreciation for being appreciated.

In some cases, teams are responsible for improving work processes, with budget savings applied to employee gain-sharing or bonuses.

All of the above can contribute to high morale, employee pride, and loyalty to the organization.

7. WHAT CHARACTERISTICS MAKE AN EXCELLENT TEAM?

With training, support, and practice, even the toughest workers can come together as an excellent team. It is important that employees understand that the purpose of the teamwork is to acknowledge the value of employee brainpower. Teamwork is for involving employees in decision-making, not for making everyone "equal" or to imply concerns about the capabilities of a supervisor. Excellent teamwork consists of teams that:

- willingly meet often, even for just a few minutes
- agree on goals and monitor them honestly
- agree on daily work procedures and assess success
- ask for opinions of other team members and other teams
- regularly receive information from organizational leaders that will help teams accomplish tasks safely and efficiently

- challenge assumptions and encourage creativity
- are asked for ideas and opinions, with organizational leaders *taking contributions seriously*
- gather, focus, and decide
- resolve differences either by agreement or compromise, or by deferring to a manager
- consult with teams in very different parts of the organization, so the right hand knows what the left hand is doing.

In some cases, team members are automatically comfortable with each other, but it is a myth that teams need to socialize and always enjoy each other's company. Camaraderie can be a nice benefit, but it is not a prerequisite to strong teamwork. Excellent teams appreciate differences and tolerate idiosyncrasies for the purpose of getting the job done.

8. WHAT ARE THE CHARACTERISTICS OF EXCELLENT TEAM MEMBERS?

You can spot good team players if they:

- listen to learn
- share what they know
- ask tough questions for the purpose of arriving at good decisions
- recognize that sometimes the team will decide and sometimes management will decide
- "pull their weight," taking their fair share of the workload
- build skills and mentor team members
- brainstorm and consider new ideas
- maintain a sense of humor about disagreements
- make every effort to resolve differences
- recognize fellow team members for their accomplishments
- are accountable for decisions, recognizing the importance of shared decision-making.

9. WHAT PHASES DO TEAMS GO THROUGH?

There are a number of descriptions of team "phases" in the litera-ture on teamwork. Although the terminology varies, the concept is the same. In successful team-building, workers develop from loosely orga-nized groups of employees into (hopefully) efficient, fully interactive teams. The rate at which they progress depends upon the makeup of the group and the degree of leadership support. If the organization is committed to the training and guidance of teams, giving them the chance to learn and apply team-building skills, the groups will have a better chance of evolving into successful teams. It is unrealistic to expect work groups to join up, instantly work together, and solve problems with minimal difficulty. Without support, they will struggle in becoming a cohesive, connected team.

The Five Phases of Teamwork

Phase One

The first phase of teamwork is when employees are initially informed about teamwork. They may be unfamiliar with the concept and wary about changes. Most employees in this phase are (under-standably) asking, "How will this affect me?" They are wondering who they will be working with, what was wrong with the "old way," and whether to believe that employees will be involved in decision-mak-ing. Employees may resist their new role, perceiving it as involving more responsibility, too much time on tasks that were traditionally the responsibility of supervisors, and more pressure to monitor work. Those employees who are the most resistant may see the development of teams as a threat to unions (what happens to seniority and job assignments?), a threat to job security, and/or an attempt to have employees "keep an eye on each other." Supervisors can be especial-ly nervous as they suspect that they will lose power and will have to forfeit responsibilities.

It is critical that senior management anticipate the fears and con-cerns of employees and repeatedly address them. A positive tone for teamwork can be set immediately by involving employees in organiz-ing the team structure, defining the expectations of teams, and clarifying how the team process will work. Emphasis should be on the commitment of leadership to supporting and guiding teams, with the understanding that adapting to the change may take a while. (Note that it is not possible to predict who will adapt the fastest. For example, sometimes long-term employees welcome a change, sometimes they do not want to budge. Sometimes new employees are willing to try anything, but other times they may resist something that they do not understand.) The themes of Phase 1 are *education* and *reassurance.*

Phase Two

The themes of Phase 2 are *planning* and *adaptation.*

In the second phase of team-building, the employees are beginning to adjust to teamwork and have begun to plan how they are going to work together. They get to know fellow team members, participate in training and team meetings, and begin to set goals. They review the organizational expectations for teams and start discussing how they can meet the expectations. They start to define their procedures and work with their supervisors to clarify how decisions will be made.

It is not unusual for teams that are humming along in Phase 2 to suddenly revert to Phase 1. For example, a team may have the responsibility for determining priorities and work assignments on a shift, after gathering information from their supervisor. Just when this process seems to be working, the supervisor shows up and gives orders without team consultation.

Oops–back to Phase 1. Time to regroup, educate, and reassure. Determine what interfered with effective teamwork and make the necessary adjustments to keep moving back to Phase 2 and on to Phase 3.

Phase Three

Once teams reach Phase 3, the themes are *comfort* and *refinement.* Teams by this time have probably survived a few battles, worked out some problems, and made some decisions that are constantly being tested. When they have reached Phase 3, they are more comfortable with the processes that they have defined, and are much more able to critique and refine the systems that they have created. For example, a team may have decided that an e-mail system can keep everyone informed. They soon discover that not everyone follows through on sending e-mail, and not everyone reads their e-mail. The team analyzes the e-mail system of communication, makes some adjustments, and tests the refined system. They clarify the expectations of team members, and determine methods for ensuring participation in the system.

Team members in Phase 3 have developed a rhythm that suits them, including meeting according to their own schedule, discussing in a manner that works for them, and monitoring goals using methods that make sense to their team.

Team members in Phase 3 have become comfortable with each other, even if they acknowledge that they like some members better than others. Skills are recognized (and weak spots are addressed by training, internships, and job assignments) and styles are appreciated. Some teams in Phase 3 may look forward to meeting for pizza after hours, but it is not necessary for teams to socialize. Phase 3 teams have figured out how different personalities, roles, experiences, and talents can combine to create the best practices and pride in work.

Phase Four

It is Phase 4 that is the ultimate goal for teams: *efficiency* and *full functioning*. Phase 4 teams routinely meet, make decisions efficiently (including budget and scheduling decisions), cross-train or distribute work assignments, work closely with supervisors and management, communicate openly, tackle problems with many points of view, work out their differences, and recognize the contributions of their coworkers. They rarely falter in their teamwork, but are not thrown if they do. They are functioning fully as a team.

Phase Five

Occasionally organizations expect their teams to reach Phase 5: *self-directed, unsupervised* teams. These teams are totally responsible for all decisions and are not supervised. (Occasionally a manager may check in, but the teams are trusted to see that all organizational goals are met on time.) Phase 5 team members may evaluate each other, determine bonuses, manage a substantial budget, and decide work flow and time frames.

Teams in Phase 5 are rare, and are usually found in small companies or in a limited number of departments of larger organizations. Their level of independence may vary, but a Phase 5 team can go for long periods of time without seeing a supervisor. Teams in Phase 5 have more decision-making responsibilities and a higher level of accountability.

It is important to note that teams do not necessarily move sequentially from Phase 1 to Phase 4 or 5 in order. In fact, a team may be new, but move quickly from Phase 2 to 3, never experiencing Phase 1. They may get stuck on Phase 3 for a while as they strive to work out systems and problems, or may quickly become fully functioning Phase 4 teams.

Another team may take longer to move from Phase 1 to Phase 2, and may need extra intervention from supervisors and senior management. Their progress may be "two steps forward, one step back" as they become more confident, experience a conflict, and require a renewal of confidence.

It would be unusual for a team to jump right into Phase 4 because it takes time to establish systems, communication strategies, and goals.

10. WHAT DO SUPERVISORS DO WHEN THERE ARE TEAMS?

Supervisors in team-based organizations are still the ultimate decision-makers. They set the tone of the organization by the way that they organize staff, relate to the teams, relay information, and set goals and expectations. They still handle the sensitive and complex issues such as crisis management, budget development, long-range planning, and personnel. They are certainly not expected to share proprietary information, or even details about public relations, marketing, and research development activities. But supervisors can inform teams in general terms about new projects, future plans, and the organization's role in the community, because access to knowledge can encourage employee support, and can assist teams in planning and in setting goals.

The primary difference for supervisors in a teamwork setting is that they are expected to consult more often with teams. Supervisors who support teamwork:

Ask employees what they think and seriously consider their ideas.
Tell employees information that will help them to do their jobs well.
Share information about the organization that would traditionally be
   limited to management meetings and boardrooms (within limits,
   of course).

While supervisors are busy gathering information and ideas from
employees, they are not giving up authority. There are basically three
types of decisions supervisors will be making in a team environment:
consultation, command, and *consensus.* There should be equal distribution
of the three types of decisions:

Consultation Decision

Supervisors in team-based environments should always be employ-
ing *consultation* as a way to make decisions. In fact, the most confident
leaders in any organization recognize that they do not know everything, and it is a good idea to consult with experts and those with more
experience in specialized areas. The supervisors and their managers
still make the final decisions, but only after gathering lots of information from employees. For supervisors of teams, it is crucial that team
members be asked about their ideas and suggestions. Supervisors
should seek out those employees with experiences or skills related to
the problem. They should gather the team together often, to decide
what to do, or to collect input before making a decision.

Command Decision

Command decisions are made when there is little room (or time) for
discussion. The supervisors give orders that must be followed. Good
supervisors in team-based organizations are often giving clear, direct
instructions with little time or opportunity for debate. *The key is that
they eventually explain the derivation of the decision.* They may have to
explain that senior management has changed priorities, a customer
has new demands, budget cuts have been made, or steps in production
need to be altered. Sometimes these explanations come hours after an
order is given, and there is no guarantee that the explanation will be
completely understood or supported by employees. But effective

teams are comfortable with following commands and getting details later, as long as they are consulted on many other decisions. The key to command decisions in a team-based organization is that teams learn the reasons behind the decision.

Consensus Decision

There is a lot written about the concept of teams reaching consensus (or 100% agreement) when they make decisions. Whenever possible, it is important for teams to discuss a problem, gather *everyone's* point of view, and then reach consensus, or full agreement, on a decision.

This process, however, can take a long time and can sometimes be impossible to achieve. The best consensus process for teams is when all perspectives are heard and everyone can live with the decision. All of the team members may not fully embrace the final decision, but they do feel as if their perspective was heard, and they can then "agree to agree." This may mean that some team members may not get their way, or may have to compromise, but as long as all team members can support the decision and all misgivings have been heard, then consensus can be achieved.

Teams that use consensus routinely have come to recognize that team members need to speak up when the team meets. Team members can undermine consensus if they withhold opinions, pretend to agree, and then refuse to support the team decision. Consensus only works if the entire team figures out how to resolve concerns that have been expressed, and then they all feel comfortable with what the entire team decides.

For consensus to be effective, supervisors need to feel confident that the team can make good decisions. Supervisors should participate in the dialogues. Sometimes supervisors use consensus as a means of asking teams if the supervisor is on the right track, or if the team has a better way to solve a problem that has been handed to the supervisor by senior management. Team consensus provides valuable support for supervisors.

Supervisors of teams should always be checking to see if their decisions have been made by *command, consensus,* or *consultation.* If they routinely mix the three, *always clarifying who is the final decision-maker,* then they can maintain their supervisory roles and still support the teamwork process.

Of course, team members need to know that their decisions may be altered or rejected as new information is presented. If the teams are *informed* and new decisions are *explained*, they will feel more confident that the organization truly supports teamwork.

11. WHAT ARE THE DRAWBACKS OF TEAMS?

Team-building is not always easy, but it can be very rewarding. Whenever a group of individuals with different personalities, styles, experiences, attitudes, work history, and training come together, it takes work for them to function together smoothly. The phases of teamwork can be a challenge for employees, especially for supervisors, but the end results can be quite positive. However, it is important to look at the drawbacks. There are three main concerns that should be addressed before a teamwork process is implemented:

The Change In Structure Can Be Disruptive.

If an organization has been structured in a traditional manner, changing to a team-based process can be a distraction. Employees will be attending more meetings and training sessions, and may be spending work time discussing the changes (or guessing about anticipated changes). Some employees may be visibly resistant, while others may lead the change, causing interpersonal conflicts. Job security may be a concern and employees may wonder about the commitment of leadership to teamwork. All of these issues can create tension, and may temporarily disrupt work flow and production.

The Change To Teamwork Takes Time.

Some organizations discover that the process of switching to a teamwork approach takes longer than expected. They may try pilot teams or extensive training before moving to an entire organizational changeover. They may see teams move from a beginning phase to a more functional phase, only to revert when a problem arises. They may encounter supervisors who find it difficult to share in decision-making, even though they have been trained in team-building and understand what is expected of them.

It is difficult to specify how long it takes to become a fully functioning team-based organization, but the minimum time frame is at least one year, and more than likely two to three years. (If it is implemented in less time, it is probably a small, congenial, enthusiastic company that gained immediate commitment to teamwork from all employees at all levels.) Organizations usually roll the process out in stages so that the structure of the organization can change without interrupting production.

The Change To Teamwork Can Require A Budget.

Expenses for team-building will vary considerably, depending upon the size of the organization, the cost of services, and the activities that are included in the teambuilding process. A budget may be required for:

- training in teamwork
- meetings
- employee(s) designated to oversee team-building
- increments for those identified as team leaders
- teamwork recognition
- bonuses, gain-sharing, team budgets, rewards, team items such as signs, T-shirts, etc. (all optional, but often used to support teamwork)
- physical plant layout changes
- team communication equipment, moving costs.

Teamwork can also suffer when goals are unclear (or not specific enough), the same problems surface and go unresolved, resources are limited (space, budget, support staff, equipment), or teams fall into "group think," focusing on unanimity and harmony, rather than on raising questions, sharing observations, and cultivating creative thinking.

12. WHAT ARE THE STEPS TO TEAMWORK?

Organizations can implement a team-based approach in many different ways, depending upon the history of the organization, the role of leadership, and the level of employee trust and involvement in change. Before designing and implementing a plan, it might be wise to consider the following steps:

• Train senior management in the concepts of teamwork. Make sure that they have debated and resolved issues related to team-building, such as the establishment and responsibilities of Team Leaders, release time for training employees, parameters to team decision-making, and rewards for effective teamwork. Establish a tentative time frame and budget guidelines.

• Gain commitment to teamwork from senior managers. Make sure they understand how they can demonstrate commitment.

• Involve employees in preparing a suggested outline of team configurations. How will the teams be organized? Will a leader be designated? Who will have decision-making authority? Will teams have Team Leaders and supervisors, or will the Team Leaders be assigned supervisory responsibilities and authority?

• Create a teamwork Steering Committee or Team-Building Task Force. Include representatives from various levels of the organizational hierarchy (front line, supervisors, union representatives, second shift, etc.) and from various skill areas. Make sure volunteers for the Steering Committee are considered. Determine the chair of the group, or establish an organizational "point person" (sometimes referred to as Teamwork Facilitator, Team-Building Manager, or Teamwork Champion) to chair the committee. Clarify steps to approval. Who approves Steering Committee decisions?

The Steering Committee should be responsible for defining team configurations, assigning employees to teams, clarifying expectations and organizational goals (for teams), and resolving other issues related to team-building. Steering Committee members should always be consulting with their coworkers, and should represent the teams. Although the Steering Committee members should not serve as mediators between teams and team members, they should be trained on how to operate as a team, especially in communicating, resolving differences, and achieving consensus.

• Inform employees about the change to teams, emphasizing that they will have representation on the Steering Committee, will be able to help design the process, and will participate in training. Be prepared to present a tentative, flexible plan that will be more finely tuned as employees provide ideas and feedback.

• Conduct introductory team training. In introductory training, participants learn about the purpose of teams, how employees can benefit from teamwork, the phases of team-building, and expectations of managers and team members. Emphasis should always be on *educating and reassuring*.

Introductory training can be done with employees in general, or after groups have been divided into teams. There are three key elements to training in teamwork:

Training should be *interactive*, allowing for practice in sharing points of view and working together.

Training should be *practical* so that participants can visualize applying teamwork to their daily work.

Training should *stress the parameters to decision-making*, reassuring participants that supervisors are still the final decision-makers, but that employees will have expanded opportunities to express ideas and share knowledge.

• Help teams to set goals. They can be simple or complex, short-term or long-term, but should be *created by the team members themselves*.

• Continue to train. Teams may be at different stages of development and may need training in topics such as:

• communication skills
• goal-setting
• conflict resolution
• facilitation
• effective meetings

Make sure supervisors and managers are included in the training with the team members.

• Recognize that expectations may vary for teams. Some teams may be expected to complete budgets and time sheets, while others are not ready for that level of responsibility. Some teams may meet two times a week, while others need to meet two times a day. Be prepared to tailor expectations to the needs of the teams.

• Meet separately with leadership. Give Team Leaders, supervisors, and managers plenty of structured time without their team members to discuss how team-building is progressing. They will need the chance to express concerns, share frustrations, identify successes, and raise questions about the future. They should create specific action steps. Emphasis should be on *education, reassurance,* and *motivation* for both the teams and leaders.

• Conduct an interim assessment of teamwork. The Steering Committee should reevaluate goals and expectations, and assess the status of teams. Were the plans and time frames realistic? Do surveys reveal weak spots and successes? Is there still confusion about roles and responsibilities? Are team members being recognized for progress? Determine priorities. Which teams need the most attention? What should be the focus of the Steering Committee in the near future? What are the biggest challenges to success?

• Troubleshoot problems as soon as they arise. The "point person" (Teamwork Facilitator, Teamwork Champion, Steering Committee chair) or other designated personnel should be prepared to intervene when teams are struggling. Steering Committee members should not serve as troubleshooters, but can look at the source of repeated problems and make adjustments to facilitate better teamwork.

• Reward and recognize teams, not only for special circumstances, but for successfully pursuing the daily work of team-building.

• Review the phases of teamwork and be prepared to see teams progress, backtrack, move forward, and struggle again. With constant communication, intervention, and support, they should achieve Phase 3 or 4.

• Keep assessing progress, making sure that teams are not compared to one another. Make changes in structure, team members, location of the team, or responsibilities, if necessary.

Remember that steps to team-building are progressive but also very flexible. As one team rapidly sets goals and achieves the goals, another team may be floundering because of temperaments and miscommunication. Intervene with those that are struggling, but do not forget to recognize those that make strong progress.

13. WHAT IS PROOF THAT TEAMWORK IS SUPPORTED BY THE ORGANIZATION?

Visible Proof

- Vision and mission statements (and perhaps even the negotiated contract!) include statements about teamwork.
- Signage, posters, and bulletin boards show open communication, promotion of teamwork, and opportunities for employee feedback.
- Steering Committee announcements are posted.
- Teams are meeting frequently, without pressure to meet.
- Charts of team goals, graphs of progress, and job assignment boards are created by teams; chalkboards have team messages.
- Senior management routinely interacts comfortably with employees.
- Team members participate in training, visit team-based organizations, and attend conferences.
- Teams have photos, banners, T-shirts, team symbols, etc. (not necessary, but fun).

Not-So-Visible Proof

- Managers are consulting informally with employees.
- Team members are participating in management meetings.
- Team members are cross-training.
- Experienced team members are mentoring new employees.
- Employees are surveyed for opinions and memos ask for feedback.
- Computer programs are designed for team record-keeping and comments.
- Team members complete paperwork without supervisory approval.
- Team members willingly assess goal progress, production levels, safety, and quality of work.
- Team members request training, meetings, and debriefings (post-project meetings) with other teams and management.

14. DO TEAMS NEED LEADERS?

If a team is not "self-directed" as in Phase 5 of team development, it might be a good idea to designate a Team Leader. The level of the leader's authority has to be established in advance of the establishment of teams. Team Leaders can be significant decision-makers, or they can serve as facilitators only. The following questions should be discussed before establishing Team Leaders:

- What will the title of leaders be? (Team Leader? Team Supervisor? Team Coordinator?)
- What will be the level of authority?
- How will Team Leaders be rewarded?
- Is it a good idea to promote a team member to Team Leader? (Not always, depending upon the past history of the employee. It is not necessarily a good idea to have the team *select* their Team Leader, either. This should be a formal personnel decision.)
- Will the Team Leaders be responsible for directions, approvals, and budgets—or will the Team Leaders simply run meetings and communicate information to managers?
- Will Team Leaders be responsible for discipline and performance reviews?
- How will Team Leaders be evaluated? (By the team?)
- Will the Team Leaders facilitate consensus and consulting but retain the power of final decision?
- What training will be provided for Team Leaders?

The role of Team Leader can be difficult at first, especially if an employee is promoted from within the organization and is suddenly leading former coworkers. It is especially difficult if the parameters of the new job are not clear. On the other hand, the promotion can be a means of recognizing employees who have demonstrated skills in communication, facilitation, and problem-solving.

Once a Team Leader is identified and the role has been clearly defined, it is a good idea for the Team Leader to move slowly in developing teamwork. The first step is for the Team Leader to discuss with the team the following questions:

- What are the teamwork expectations
    of the organization?
    of the Team Leader?
    of the team members as a team?
    of the team members as individuals?
- How will the team measure whether those expectations are being met?
- What will be the ground rules for functioning as a team?
- Who will be the liaison to other teams?
- Who in the organization will provide input to the team?
- What training is needed by the team?
- What assistance can be provided in goal development?

Team Leaders should participate in training related to facilitation skills, problem-solving, communication strategies, and conflict resolution. Excellent Team Leaders model listening, trust, information-sharing, and constant positive recognition of team members. They are willing to ask difficult questions and encourage teams to constantly assess their progress as a team. The best Team Leaders are always consulting with both the team and management and are always focusing on solving problems, especially under stressful conditions such as tight deadlines or interpersonal tensions within the team.

15. WHY WOULD TEAMWORK FAIL?

Team-building may suffer from fits and starts as employees become adjusted to the concept and experiment with ways to improve their teamwork. There will be moments when employees (especially managers) will want to throw their hands in the air and shout, "It's not working"! but the beauty of teamwork is that when these moments occur, employees as a team can put their heads together and figure out how to get back on track. Success is not dependent upon one person's solutions or leadership. There is always support available from the team members if motivation and problem-solving are needed.

However, teamwork can fail if:

Senior Management Does Not Demonstrate Commitment.

If senior leaders claim to support teamwork but constantly give orders with little discussion, never ask employees about their ideas, refuse to share organizational plans and goals, and generally maintain a traditional "us-versus-them" role, then teamwork will eventually fail. The best way to counteract this problem is to clarify *exactly* how senior leaders can demonstrate commitment. Be specific. Senior leaders should be visible, sharing information, and constantly asking for input and feedback.

Contract Negotiations Do Not Address The Teamwork Process.

Although organizations have managed to conduct successful negotiations and contract development in a team-based environment, it takes trust to openly share information and arrive at a consensus. If contractual difficulties develop, teamwork may fail—or at least flounder—until there is successful resolution.

But contractual difficulties do not necessarily mean that strong teamwork is not possible. Sometimes conflicts during negotiations are misinterpreted as an indication that employees cannot work together as teams. The best way to counteract this problem is to determine at the outset what the process will be for reaching negotiated conclusions in a team-based workplace. Negotiators on both sides should recognize that problems such as disagreements or the guarding of information do not automatically imply that teamwork has failed. Contract development is an extremely stressful process. Tempers can flare, heels can dig in, and information can be a valuable commodity. If it is established at the beginning that the dialogue is not personal and will result in fair-minded compromise, then that goal should be repeated constantly. Negotiations can be conducted so that the concepts and purpose of teamwork can be maintained. Some contracts will specify how teams will function, providing valuable teamwork guidelines for the future.

Influential Employees Can Undermine Teamwork.

If teamwork is a brand-new concept and employees are wary and uncertain, then it is important to spend time with employees who are negative, especially if they are particularly influential. These employees may be union leaders, long-term employees, well-respected vocal workers, or simply those who love to raise questions and get discussions going. In many cases, their concerns are legitimate and they are willing to say out loud what others are thinking. It is important to address the issues that they bring up, or, better yet, anticipate the questions that they will raise. (The questions generally center around job security, job responsibilities and expectations, promotions, union support, team groupings, contract compliance, and rewards and recognition.)

However, on occasion, the influential employees may attempt to sabotage the team-building process by suggesting negative implications to teamwork, spreading rumors, and maintaining minimal participation in team-building activities. If they are able to successfully sway others, teamwork may fail.

The best approach to counteracting employees who want to undermine teamwork is to work with them personally on developing cooperation and commitment. Some employees may need a longer time to adjust and may need to maintain their sense of influence. They may need coaching in how to be a contributing team member. They do not want to lose their status in the organization and may have to be invited to serve as a designated "devil's advocate" who raises important questions that should be discussed. Often the most negative employees just want to be heard, and want to be treated as valued contributors to Steering Committee meetings and team training sessions. They can be easily ignored if the style of their comments overshadows the message. They do not want to be disregarded, even if they are raising questions that appear to disrupt progress. They may be expressing what others are thinking and need a chance to speak their minds. Once taken seriously, their influence can become positive. If limits are established, the most negative employees can turn out to be significant leaders in team-building because they can maintain their influence and still be heard.

However, it may be necessary to discipline disruptive employees if they become insubordinate or violate policies. (Expressing views is an important part of teamwork, but not when the results can be a violation of organizational policies.)

It is extremely important to concentrate on the majority of the employees who are making an effort to achieve successful teamwork.

Encourage those who work hard. Reward progress and promote successes. Those few employees who hold back may start to feel left behind, and, hopefully, will want to join in and use their influence in a more positive manner.

16. WHAT HAPPENS IN TEAM MEETINGS?

Team meetings do not have to be long, daily sessions with an agenda, scribe, and timekeeper. They can be two minutes long if the team can efficiently resolve a question in that time. They can be three times a day or three times a week. They can have a standard format, or change depending upon circumstances.

The most important element of team meetings is that they should be worth every minute. In other words, there is no set formula to the team meeting.

Four Types of Team Meetings

1. Information meetings, consisting of:

   • new information
   • work distribution
   • changes in priorities
   • announcements
   • quick problem-solving
   • status updates

Information meetings are often quick and to the point, run by team members or the Team Leader.

2. Planning meetings, consisting of:

   • goal-setting
   • timeline development
   • budget review
   • project planning

Planning meetings usually require facilitation and minutes.

  3. Team-building meetings, consisting of:

   • training (varying from intensive goal-setting to "adventure" experiences, trust-building exercises, and interpersonal skills)
   • conflict resolution
   • teamwork assessments
   • goal assessment

Team-building meetings usually require experienced trainers.

  4. Debriefing meetings, consisting of:

   • post-project review
   • post-goal achievement
   • post-project problem-solving
   • planning for future work phases
   • celebrations

Debriefing meetings usually require facilitation.

  When organizing team meetings, the teams should decide:

  • How often do we need to meet to make sure that everyone is informed and up-to-date?
  • What is the purpose of our meetings?
  • Do we have to physically meet together or are there alternative methods of connecting (handheld radios, teleconferences, e-mail, etc.)?
  • Can anyone call a meeting?
  • Who starts, facilitates, times, and ends the meetings?
  • Does everyone always need to be there?
  • How will we communicate between meetings?
  • Who else outside the team should participate?
  • Where should the meetings be held?
  • How will we remember what we decided?
  • What if attendance is poor?
  • What if we have very few items to discuss?

- What if we cannot cover everything that needs to be discussed?
- What if we spend too much time discussing and not enough time deciding?
- What if a team member disrupts a meeting?
- What if we keep failing to meet?
- How can we conduct a "mood check" (attitudes, dynamics, treatment, etc.)?
- How can we make sure that our meetings are worth the time?

It is important to take time to assess the effectiveness of the team meetings. Many teams discover that their 10-minute meetings twice a day are far more effective than daily 20-minute meetings because of time constraints, attention span, and the quality of meeting facilitation.

17. SHOULD TEAMS MAKE FINAL DECISIONS?

It is important that team members be aware of the different types of decisions that supervisors and managers will be making in a team-based organization. When an organization restructures to teams, it does not mean that teams are suddenly "empowered" to run the organization. In fact, "empowerment" in business means that employees share in the decision-making process and have the opportunity to provide insights and feedback. It does not mean that they have the "power" to make all decisions. The ultimate decision-making power still rests with the leaders of the organization.

It is important that the parameters of decision-making are established before team-building is implemented. For some decisions, teams will have little or no input (but decisions will be revealed and explained). For other decisions, they will be consulted for expertise and advice, but management will make the final decision. (The managers will often be privy to information that cannot be shared with employees for privacy or legal reasons.) In many cases, the teams will have full decision-making power and will be trusted to use their expertise to make a decision, seeking out assistance if needed. Sometimes teams will reach consensus (100% agreement) or they may agree to pass along a decision for the final approval of a supervisor.

A strong team-based organization has many different types of decision-making occurring every day. It is vital that team members are comfortable with their role in the process, and managers understand that organizational leaders can make better decisions if they gather information and suggestions.

18. HOW DOES A TEAM KNOW HOW WELL IT'S DOING?

Teams can assess their progress by:

- routinely discussing teamwork during team meetings (which may mean someone has to bring up sensitive issues)
- inviting observers to provide feedback
- creating a self-assessment tool that is reviewed on a regular basis
- checking on goal achievement
- participating in anonymous surveys that are summarized by personnel outside the team
- recording and posting progress and accomplishments.

It is not advisable for team members to evaluate each other unless they are quite willing to be honest about personal observations and discuss them openly, without fear of jeopardizing team member relationships. (Such openness is rare.) Standard performance reviews that include team member assessments should be implemented by the Human Resources/Personnel Department and supervisors.

Chapter 3

THE TRUTH ABOUT INTERVIEWING

Remind me again, who are we interviewing today?
(Plant Safety Supervisor, five minutes before the first candidate arrives.)

Supervisors spend most of their work time guiding employees. They set goals and standards, provide instruction and assistance, and facilitate productivity and job satisfaction. These activities require constant communication in the form of group meetings, individual consultation, and informal discussion and socializing. The quality of the communication depends not only upon the skills and efforts of the supervisors, but upon the skills and attitudes of the employees.

That is precisely why effective interviewing of potential employees is so important. Job interviews are pivotal in determining who will best offer strong skills and a positive attitude to the organization. Job interviews, if conducted professionally, can be the key factor in determining who will bring value to an organization and who will work well with future coworkers and supervisors. If job interviews are taken seriously, with thorough preparation, an organized process, and complete follow through, then supervisors will obtain valuable information so that they can make better decisions about who should join the organization. The supervisors will know what to expect from a new hire because they have been part of the process in identifying the best person for the job.

Supervisors who take the time to learn about candidates during an interview will be aware of the skills, style, and interests of a new employee. If the philosophy and goals of the organization are discussed in the interview, the new employee is already well informed about expectations, and has made a decision to join the organization in achieving the goals.

Supervisors usually do not have a lot of time to conduct interviews, but later they will spend even more time coaching, counseling, and disciplining the wrong hire if they do not find the time for a thorough interview process.

This chapter provides realistic information about how supervisors can conduct successful interviews, including suggestions about how to prepare, how to gather essential information, and how to make fair and unbiased decisions.

1. WHAT IS THE PURPOSE OF INTERVIEWING?

After a job has been advertised and the initial screening of applications has taken place, it is a good idea to invite candidates in to the organization for an interview. Job interviews give both the organization and the candidates a chance to gather more information that can help with employment choices. There are several important reasons for conducting interviews:

Presentation Assessment

The interview is an opportunity to gain a sense of the style of candidates. Skills and experience are often listed on a resume or job application, but how the candidate provides information, communicates attitudes, and articulates goals and aspirations can provide valuable data for making a decision. The interview is the chance to see the approach of the candidates to solving problems. It can reveal actual knowledge of the work, initiative on the job, research conducted prior to the interview, as well as professionalism and work ethic. If interview questions are designed properly, the candidates will not only respond to what is being asked but also reveal behavioral characteristics and personal qualities that will influence hiring decisions.

Comfortable Elaboration

One of the purposes of an interview is to encourage candidates to elaborate upon written materials, whether the materials are in the form of a letter, resume, or organizational application. The interview gives applicants a chance to explain, provide details, and brag a bit.

Candidates are more willing to share information if they are relaxed and comfortable. If they are treated with respect and made to feel at ease, they will be more inclined to talk comfortably about themselves.

It is *not* the purpose of an interview to create stress and intimidation. Some interviewers feel that a "stress interview" (or a "good cop-bad cop" approach) will be the best way to find out how a candidate handles pressure. Unfortunately, a tense interview does not give the candidate a chance to openly share information because there is a tendency to try to guess what is expected, or anxiety interferes with concentration and the ability to communicate. If the workplace is fast-paced and high-pressured, then the candidates should have the opportunity to give examples of how they have handled similar work experiences and how they have reacted to stress. An interview is stressful enough. If the interviewers are aggressive and unresponsive, it sends a message about future coworkers more than information about the work of the organization.

If interviewers need to know more about the ability of the candidates to handle the pressure of work-related stresses such as closing a deal, coping with a difficult customer, or working against a tight deadline, it is better to describe scenarios and listen carefully to the reactions of the candidates. Do they relish the challenge? Have they already developed tactics for handling stress? Have they been in similar situations? If so, what did they learn? If not, how would they approach a new situation that they have been told might be stressful?

This approach not only assists interviewers in learning more about the candidates, it gives a better impression of the organization. Good candidates who experience a "stress interview" may decide that they would prefer not to work in an environment that uses pressure tactics.

Job Details

One of the main reasons for an interview is for interviewers to explain the details of the job. A written job description may be vague or unclear (or nonexistent). Part of an interview should be devoted to a summary of the job responsibilities, including work hours, overtime possibilities, occasional unique responsibilities, certification and examination requirements, location in the hierarchy, and opportunities for advancement.

Candidates should learn the job details early in the interview. A lot of time can be saved if candidates can link their responses to the specific job responsibilities, or if they can determine immediately that the job is not what they expected it to be.

Organizational Impressions

The interview is not just for finding out about the candidates. The interview can be the best chance for the candidates to make decisions about the organization. It is important to remember that the candidates are also forming impressions.

Confirm Concerns

Every once in a while there are "red flags" in application materials that require further investigation. It may be a gap in time on the resume, a job title that does not match a job description, or an unfinished degree or certification. There may be reasonable explanations for questionable application information. An interview is a good time to show that all aspects of an application are seriously reviewed, and that the organization is giving candidates a chance to explain.

Break Down Fakes

Candidates can write some amazing information on paper. In fact, they can write half-truths and outright lies. An interview is a chance to determine the accuracy of the descriptions on resumes and application forms. Did the candidate *direct* a project or serve on the committee? A professional certification was completed, but was it kept up-to-date? Why was attendance at Harvard for three years?

If questions are framed properly and application materials reviewed thoroughly, the interview can be used to determine veracity and to gather background information.

Better Job Placement

On occasion, candidates are interviewed and it becomes clear that there may be a more appropriate position in the organization. For example, a candidate may apply for a position as a customer service representative, but responses to questions (as well as interview behavior) indicate that a position in sales may be a better match. The written resume provides only part of the picture of the capabilities of candidates.

Sense Enthusiasm

Interviews are a chance for candidates to reveal their attitude about the job. They can convey their interest by doing research on the organization, preparing questions, answering questions carefully, presenting a professional appearance, and expressing genuine enthusiasm for the job. These qualities do not necessarily come through in a cover letter or job application, and can profoundly influence hiring decisions.

Interviewing job applicants is only one part of a complete hiring package. The hiring process should not stop when final candidates have been selected. References should be checked thoroughly. Information on the resume should be researched for verification. Once the candidate has been hired, training and orientation sessions should be conducted so that the new employee can be successful. Even if new candidates are impressive on paper and shine during an interview, it is the follow-up from the first day of work that will ensure that good hiring decisions were made.

2. WHO SHOULD CONDUCT THE INTERVIEW?

Although there are several configurations of the interview process, the following three formats work effectively. The actual format will be determined by scheduling, staff availability, type of job, number of candidates, interviewer, and role of senior management in hiring.

Interview Team

Although a team of interviewers can sometimes be intimidating to the candidate, the process can be effective if carried out properly. The candidates should be informed in advance that there will be a team of interviewers. (There should be no more than four interviewers to save time and reduce candidate stress!) Explain the format of the interview, especially if one interviewer is not participating other than to observe or take notes. All of the interviewers should make a point to help the candidate feel comfortable by explaining their roles in the organization and by asking questions that show that application and resume have been reviewed in advance.

In a team interview, preplanning is essential. The interviewers should plan questions, discuss the order of the questions, determine time frames, and prearrange signals for either pursuing a topic or ending the interview. They should determine follow-up steps and know ahead of time who will make the final decision.

Candidates will often try to determine who is the most influential person in the interview, or who will be their future supervisor. Explain that all candidates will experience the same interview process, and that all of the interviewers will be involved in the decision-making process. (There is no need to specify who makes the actual decision.) Make sure that all of the interviewers are invited to share feedback after the interviews, even if they do not make the final selection.

The team interview can be informative for the candidates. They can get a sense of the tone of the organization, the camaraderie of coworkers, and the organization's ability to plan and carry out the hiring process. If the team is unprepared, harried, or joking, candidates can get a negative impression of the organization.

Once candidates are informed about the process of the team interview, it is easier for them to relax and answer questions. Do not jump around, hitting the candidate with questions from all sides. The interview process is intended to learn about the candidates, not to shut down communication and create stress.

Interview Pair

A pair of interviewers is an efficient way to conduct a series of interviews because the process saves time and allows for a comparison of observations. The ideal arrangement is to assign the same two interviewers to all of the interviews so that both interviewers are well informed about all of the candidates. They may have very different perceptions of the candidates, and can compare notes afterward.

Two interviewers can take turns asking prearranged questions, with either interviewer following up with additional questions. The candidates may not feel as overwhelmed as when there is a team of interviewers.

It is quite effective to pair up interviewers from different departments, levels, or skill areas. They may make different observations during the interviews, but may end up drawing the same conclusions.

Try to select interviewers who have different styles. For example, one interviewer may be relaxed and outgoing and the other more formal and businesslike. The candidates need to be able to work with many different styles at work, and how they respond to styles can be quite revealing.

When the pair of interviewers agree on a finalist, a second interview may be necessary for confirmation and job offers. If the two interviewers are not in agreement, it is helpful to a third interviewer to hear *all* of the interviewer observations *ahead of time*, so that the appropriate questions can be designed to gain a thorough picture of the candidate.

Single Interviewer

One interviewer can be responsible for the initial screening or the full interview, but it is advisable to get additional perspectives from other employees. The single interviewer may be either a Human Resources/Personnel representative, or a supervisor of the potential employee. One interviewer can invite a coworker to drop in at the end of the interview to verify impressions later. Or, if the candidate appears to be a possible hire, then a second interview may be held with a representative from a higher level in the organization or from the department where the employee will be working.

Occasionally, a coworker at the same level as the potential hire will conduct the initial interview. For example, if a welder is being interviewed, the organization may prefer that the initial interviewer also be a welder who will know if the interview answers are correct. (Employees who will be participating in interviews should always be trained in interviewing skills.)

Single interviewers may feel uncomfortable because they are the sole source of information about the candidates. Consultation with coworkers after the interview may help the interviewer to feel more confident about a recommendation. It may be determined that another employee needs to conduct a second interview.

In some organizations, a senior manager, the business owner, or the chief executive officer of the company are responsible for the final say in hiring, even if they have not participated in interviews. Whether interviewers choose the finalists or not, they should know that their primary purpose is to gather as much information from candidates as possible, so that successful choices can be made.

3. HOW SHOULD THE INTERVIEW BE CONDUCTED?

Interviews are most helpful to both the candidates and the interviewers if they are well planned. Candidates will feel more relaxed if they feel that the interviewers did their homework and are genuinely interested in them. When they are comfortable, they can answer questions more openly and reveal valuable information.

The design of the interview should allow for candidates to do most of the talking. To make candidates feel at ease, consider the setting and the format of the interview. For example:

- Sit around a table. Do not put candidates in a low, soft chair, especially if they are seated lower than the interviewer. Do not stand when candidates are seated, or sit on the edge of a desk or table.
- It may seem polite to offer coffee or a soft drink, but candidates have indicated that they do not know what to do with the cup. They are afraid they will spill the drink, or that their hands will shake.
- Do not keep candidates waiting long. Provide materials about the organization for them to read, but make sure that candidates are waiting where they do not feel as if they are being observed and cannot overhear office conversations. If several candidates are scheduled, try to arrange it so that they do not have to sit and wait together.
- Do not blindside candidates with a team of interviewers. Inform them ahead of time about who will be interviewing them. Explain the role of each interviewer, especially if someone is there to take notes.
- Make sure reasonable accommodations have been made, using the guidelines from the Americans with Disabilities Act (ADA).

• Do not videotape or tape an interview unless you have checked with the legal department and have received the written consent of the candidates.

Suggested Process for Conducting an Informative Interview

1. Make A Positive Impression

Be prepared and plan with cointerviewers.
Allow uninterrupted time.
Read the application materials ahead of time.
Highlight areas that you want to ask about.
Prepare specific questions that are the same for all candidates, plus possible follow-up questions that are specifically about the applications.
Choose a quiet location for the candidates to wait.
Greet the candidates; put them at ease.
Candidates should not "cross paths."
Make sure the candidates cannot overhear conversations about the organization or the interview process. Make the interview comfortable and private.
Remember that candidates draw conclusions about the workplace on the basis of how they are treated and what they observe during the time of their visit.

2. Set Up Signals

Prior to the interview, discuss with cointerviewers why an interview may have to be ended early and how to end it.

Sometimes candidates say something that an interviewer determines is a reason for rejecting a candidate, or is conflicting information. Set up signals if an interviewer wants to pursue a question or a topic without making it obvious to the candidate, or wants to end the interview. (Possible signals: move a pen, rub chin, turn over a piece of paper.)

3. Provide Background

Begin by providing background information on the organization, using a chart or other visuals that are easy to understand. Spend no more than three or four minutes talking about the organization.

Describe the job briefly, emphasizing the daily tasks. Make sure to mention scheduling and special job requirements such as certifications, so that the candidates can determine immediately if they are still interested in the job.

Do not "sell" the position, even if a candidate is the clear first choice. Continue through the interview process to validate impressions.

Do not discuss salary and benefits at the beginning of the interview. (It may be necessary to provide an answer if the candidate asks, but get right back to the interview questions. A salary answer does not have to be specfic.)

After providing background information confirm that the candidates are still interested in the position.

4. Explain Interview Format

Be vague when explaining the agenda for the interview. Use the same format for everyone, but do not specify the amount of time each section (or the entire interview) will take. For some candidates you will want more time, for others you may end the interview early.

A suggested format is a brief overview of the organization and the job, followed by a series of prepared questions that interviewers have preplanned, with occasional follow-up questions.

Interviews are more effective if the candidates are encouraged to ask questions at any time. This reveals curiosity, thought processes, motivation, ability to acquire information, and other qualities. Interviews should consist of the interviewers talking less than 25 percent of the time.

If there is a team of interviewers, one person should keep track of how much time is left for completing the interview.

5. Ask Prearranged Questions And Follow-Up Questions

Details about interview questions are provided later in this chapter, but, in general, questions should be distributed among interviewers ahead of time. To keep track of time, limit interviewers to one or two follow-up questions. If there is only one interviewer, make sure that questions are checked off as they are asked. It is not essential that they be asked in order, but keeping track will ensure that all candidates will be presented with the same basic questions.

If candidates do not seem to be forthcoming, it may be the setting and tone of the interview, or it may be the design of the questions. (It could also be a shy or evasive candidate, but all effort should be made to help the candidate feel comfortable enough to share information.) Begin with easy, relaxed questions that center around the job tasks and the training and experience that may be related. Later in the interview, ask the problem-solving, open-ended questions. Try not to hit the candidates with sudden, unexpected challenges, especially in the beginning of the interview. This just adds to the stress and may inhibit the candidates.

Some candidates are more than willing to talk. They may talk so much that they never actually answer the question. Do not hesitate to repeat a question or a variation of the question to encourage the candidates to focus. Paraphrase an answer to confirm that it was understood. Recognize that some answers are deliberately long and confusing because the candidates do not know what to say.

6. Listen And Take Notes

The primary purpose of interview notes is to show respect for the candidates. Note-taking not only helps interviewers to remember what transpired, but it also informs the candidates that their words were worth recording. It may seem unnecessary if there will be a small number of interviews, but even two interviews can begin to blur together and information can be forgotten.

Being able to refer to notes is especially helpful after a series of interviews or when there is a long break between interviews. Since notes might be used later as legal documentation of whether an interview was conducted fairly, the contents of the notes should be brief, factual, and written for the purpose of later reminders.

Write notes about the candidate's answers, not personal reactions of the interviewers.

Candidates are sometimes uncomfortable when interviewers take lots of notes. They watch to see what the interviewers write down and can occasionally read what has been written. Explain that notes will be taken so that the responses of the candidates will be recalled accurately. Do not concentrate on the note-taking but on maintaining eye contact with the candidate.

Create abbreviations so that information can be recorded quietly and privately. For example, if the candidate arrived late, make an "L" on the notes. If there are concerns about time management skills, do not write notes about time management, but jot down reminders about answers that were clues about time management. For example, if a candidate explains that more time was required to finish two major projects, the interviewers should write "late projs–needed more time" rather than "poor time management. "

Good notes will jog the memories of interviewers about their observations and concerns, allowing for further review and contemplation. Avoid quick judgments, and do not record conclusions made in the interview. Once a post-interview conference is held to discuss all of the interviews, the notes should be clear enough so that decisions are objective and accurate.

Record what is important to remember. Exact wording, specific quotes and phrases, and relevant facts should be written in notes. For example, if the candidate completed training that no other candidates have, write it down. If the candidate shows unusual enthusiasm, write down what the candidate said or did that showed enthusiasm, such as presenting a work sample, asking prepared questions about the job, or expressing a clear desire to work for the organization. If the candidate comments, "I hate getting everything done at the last minute," or "I work best when there is a sudden deadline," the interviewers should record those comments. Never assume that the details about the interview will be remembered. Take notes.

7. Question Interviewer Conclusions

Be careful not to jump to conclusions during an interview. Interviewers could be wrong, especially if they base their conclusions on:

- first impressions
- erroneous assumptions
- unintentional biases.

Interviewers should ask themselves: What evidence do I have to back up my conclusions about a candidate? Question the initial judgment to determine whether there are facts to support the reactions.

All interviewers should be aware of how they may be unintentionally influenced during an interview. Stereotyping and bias can not only rule out valid candidates, but can result in discrimination.

Stereotyping = drawing conclusions based on preconceived notions about color, age, dress, language, gender, religion, mannerisms, and other factors
Example: Assuming that women are not very good in math.
Bias = acting upon those stereotypes, such as making assumptions about skill levels, work ethic, attitude, etc., and forming questions or tasks around those biases to verify the stereotype
Example: Asking only the female candidates to work out difficult math problems under pressure.
Discrimination = acting upon stereotypes illegally
Example: Not opening a position that requires math to women because of the assumption that women are not good at math

8. Gather, Then Sell, Then Explain Next Steps

Know ahead of time if interviewers can make a job offer. Never suggest to candidates that they are "in the running," "at the top of the list," or "the best so far."

Get answers to questions first, before selling the job. Set up a prearranged system for determining whether the interviewers should begin to try to "sell" the job. Do not express significant enthusiasm or make promises, even if the candidate is clearly the best choice.

Avoid making negative statements about the organization, even in a joking fashion:

• Are you sure you want to work for this place?
• We only gave you the good side!

Do give a realistic picture:

• We just went through a merger and there are more changes ahead.

- The job you are applying for may be transferred to our satellite site. We should know by November.
- This job can be stressful at times because the workload is demanding. It eases up in the summer, and picks up again in September.

Be careful about giving the wrong impression about possibilities such as higher pay, nearby parking, promotions, etc. If benefits are part of an overall employee development plan, then share the information, but do not project or make promises.

Explain to the candidates what will happen after the interviews are completed. Give approximate time frames and make sure that the candidates know the name of a contact person should they have further questions.

4. WHAT SHOULD BE DONE BEFORE AN INTERVIEW?

Pre-interview planning can make the difference between an unproductive interview and an interview that provides valuable information. Once candidates have been selected to be interviewed:

- Establish clear criteria for final selection. What are you looking for?
- Reserve a quiet, private room. Inform employees that interviews are not to be interrupted.
- Determine who will conduct the interviews.
- Schedule so that there are no more than four interviews in one day, if possible. Consider how the time of day will affect the interview process for both the candidates and the interviewers. Allow at least one hour for conducting the interview, organizing notes afterward, and preparing for the next interview. (This may seem like too much time out of a busy day, but it is a realistic time frame if the process is to be taken seriously.)
- Determine when interviewers will meet to discuss their impressions of the candidates. Although it is difficult, immediate reactions may be shared quickly, but thorough discussions should not occur until all candidates have been interviewed.
- Check out the setting and interview arrangements to make sure that they allow for schedule flow, candidate privacy, access to the

facility, availability of personnel for tours and second interviews, and appropriate seating. (Candidates can be asked if accommodations such as parking, elevator, or ramp entrances need to be accessible for the interview, but ask *all* candidates the same question.)

- Determine standard questions that will be asked of every candidate, tailoring them to match the job description and the criteria for selection.
- Review all application materials, highlighting key areas and topics for   follow-up questions. Write down the questions.
- Determine the format of the interview, including:

  - who will give an overview of the organization and the job
  - the order that the questions will be asked
  - how the tone will be established
  - how time will be monitored
  - who might observe or take notes
  - what signals need to be established
  - who can make a job offer
  - what follow-up steps will be implemented.

- Gather visuals that provide information on the organization and the job.
- Review the note-taking process.
- Review policies and regulations related to legal questions, Americans with Disabilities Act (ADA) procedures, and other guidelines for conducting fair and unbiased interviews. (See sample questions later in this chapter.)
- Find out whether candidates need accommodations for parking, building access, or room setting.
- Determine post-interview timelines and stick to them, especially if candidates are waiting to hear if they are still a potential hire. If there have been hiring delays or changes, inform all candidates.

5. WHAT INFLUENCES INTERVIEWERS?

Interviewers can be easily influenced by their first impressions and by their own personal biases. Laws have been developed to protect candidates from deliberate or unintentional bias and discrimination. Even if interviewers try to approach interviews with an unbiased, open mind, there are always preconceived notions and stereotypes that can influence decisions. What do you think would influence you if you were interviewing a candidate? (Be honest!)

You may have responded with basic "first impressions" such as:

- appearance
- handshake
- hygiene
- demeanor (fidgety, confident, harried, friendly, funny, stern, silly, etc.)
- height or weight.

Once the immediate reactions take place, it is often hard for interviewers to ignore their initial perceptions. But it is crucial that interviewers refrain from jumping to conclusions. Use the interviews to get fresh evaluations. In many cases, the initial reactions to candidates are incorrect. Interviewers should keep asking themselves if they are being unduly influenced by irrelevant factors and their own personal biases.

Remember:

- People exhibit unusual mannerisms when they are nervous, such as laughing, hesitating, or chattering. Sometimes nervousness is an indication that the candidate really wants the job, so listen carefully to what the candidate has to say. Concentrate on finding evidence that will change the initial first impression, even if it is an initial *good* impression. (For example, a candidate may have done considerable research on the organization, but may not have the appropriate credentials for the job. The initial reaction of the interviewers may be positive and impressed, forgetting that specific credentials are required.) Candidates should not be classified on the basis of their appearance or mannerisms, even if the classifying may seem to be in their favor. Base conclusions on matching skills to the job.
- Friendliness can mask inability to concentrate on a task. Be careful about being influenced by an outgoing personality, quick wit, or exceptional vocabulary. Do these qualities fit the criteria for selection?

- Focus on tough questions that hone in on skills and work habits.
- Flashy or unusual dress could indicate an earnest desire to impress, or the candidates may have misunderstood the tone of the organization. The candidates may either change the mode of dress to fit in, or may continue to exhibit a personal, unique style. Ask yourself if the choice of clothing really matters. If a candidate is well qualified for the job, a second interview may reveal the ability of the candidate to assess the work environment and dress appropriately.
- Long, detailed responses could indicate a desire to avoid the actual question. Rephrase the question or point out that the actual question was not answered, giving the candidates another chance to provide an answer.
- Short, uninformative responses could be an indication that the candidates are so nervous that they are unable to think of the answers to the questions. Start with something easy and obvious to get candidates relaxed.
- A series of questions from the candidates may not indicate enthusiasm and curiosity, but a desire to avoid providing information. Inform the candidates of the time frame and keep control of the interview.
- A comment that may sound sarcastic or critical could be an innocent attempt to make small talk. For example, if the candidates comment on the noise level of the office or the length of the wait, it may not be a complaint but a nervous effort to connect with the interviewer. Do not let candidates feel as if they "got off on the wrong foot." Give them plenty of opportunities to recover from mistakes and to reveal their true qualities.
- Cases of bias and discrimination in interviews are well documented. The best candidates can be lost because of the prejudices of interviewers. Laws exist to protect the candidates and to protect the agency from mistakes that could be made by biased interviewers. (This does not preclude organizations from establishing clear policies about bias and discrimination, and from ensuring that interviewers are trained on how to conduct a fair and informative interview.)

Laws such as the Age Discrimination in Employment Act (ADEA), Title I and Title V of the Americans with Disabilities Act, state human rights laws, Title VII of the Civil Rights Act of

1964, and other laws and legislation provide important information for interviewers. If unsure about the legal aspects of rejecting a candidate, consult with the organization's legal representation or Human Resources/Personnel. New legal decisions about employment are being made every day.

Occasionally, it is difficult to determine if an assumption about a candidate is accurate. "Self-identity" refers to information that is provided voluntarily by the candidate, such as information about childcare concerns, or disabilities that are not obvious. Interviewers should be careful that they do not ask questions to seek out information that may be irrelevant or illegal to pursue. Make sure that questions relate to actual work identified in a job description. "Bona fide" questions are those questions that have a direct link to the work of the job. Interviewers should ask themselves what really will affect the ability of the candidates to fulfill the job responsibilities. For example, the possible negative reactions of future coworkers, or possible difficulties with fitting into the existing culture, should not be relevant when determining whether candidates have the skills to do the job and are viable candidates.

• Interviewers may not only be influenced by the candidate, but by the interview process itself. For example, the following factors can influence the attitude of the interviewers:

• the time of day of the interview
• outside pressures causing a distraction
• previous candidates who left a strong impression
• personal level of influence in final decision-making
• tight schedules
• the number of interviews in a row
• sympathy, friendship, empathy, and other emotions
• lack of confidence in interviewing.

These factors should be considered during the pre-interview planning process, with changes made to esure fair and informative interviews.

6. WHAT ARE THE BASIC GUIDELINES FOR INTERVIEW QUESTIONS?

When determining what to ask in an interview so that questions are legal and appropriate, follow these four guidelines:

1. Plan Questions In Advance

Review the job requirements and the characteristics needed to fulfill the job responsibilities. Create questions that are basic background questions, asked of every candidate. Discuss the questions with cointerviewers, supervisors, Human Resources/Personnel, and legal representatives of the organization. Various federal, state, and local laws regulate some of the questions that can be asked on a job application, in an interview, and during testing. If the question does not seem related to fulfilling the functions of the job, delete the question. Job-related questions are tied to:

- the purpose of the job
- what the job holder actually does
- how the person performs the job
- what interpersonal skills are required
- what work skills/training are required
- any unique skills or characteristics that may be required.

Physical attributes may be required if they are a bona fide job qualification. ("Bona fide" refers to job qualifications that can be shown to be essential to carrying out the job, such as lifting, pushing, driving, climbing, and so forth.)

2. Follow Up

Standard questions asked of everyone may require follow-up questions for clarification or further elaboration. Before asking an additional question, consider whether the question is based on a true need for more information that will contribute to a decision. Why is the question being asked? Make sure that follow-up questions are tied to something that a candidate said. It shows that interviewers have been listening, and encourages elaboration. Use questions that require more than a "yes" or "no." Examples are:

- Why (did you decide to pursue a job here)?
- How (did you get your previous jobs)?
- What (do you think that you would like about this job)?
- Which (of your work experiences did you like best)?
- What (have you accomplished that you are proud of)?

Additional questions are not as specific, and leave it completely up to the candidate to provide further information:

- Can you elaborate?
- How so?
- Why was that?
- In what sense?
- Why do you think that happened?

3. Reconsider Questions

If interviewers are considering whether a question is appropriate, they *should not ask it.* (If in doubt, do not ask.) If the answer may be related to the job, take time to figure out how to rephrase the question.

4. Listen To The Answers

Candidates can usually tell if interviewers are paying attention. Make sure questions are not repeated or rephrased later. Most important, listen carefully to the wording of the responses. Sometimes a vague question may prompt a lengthy and revealing response. If candidates seem satisfied with their responses, their attitude can sometimes be more revealing than the content of the answer.

7. WHAT QUESTIONS SHOULD NEVER BE ASKED?

Various federal, state, and local laws regulate some of the questions that can be asked on a job application, in an interview, or during testing. Questions should always be related to carrying out the functions of the job.

Before conducting an interview, prepare questions ahead of time and have them reviewed by Human Resources/Personnel or by legal representation of the organization. It is inevitable that additional questions will be asked during the interview, mostly for the purpose of clarification or to gather more information. Interviewers should be well versed on what questions should not be asked because the questions may be biased or illegal. Before asking any questions, the interviewer should think, "Is this question truly related to the job?" If a cointerviewer is concerned about a question, then a rephrasing should be done immediately, without saying, "You do not have to answer that" or "We cannot ask that. " Interject with "Let me rephrase that so that the question is clear. . . ."

The Following Questions Should Not Be Asked During The Interviews:

Family Status

Marital history or status

Name or employment of spouse

Maiden name

Names, number, ages of children

Pregnancy or plans for childbearing

Childcare arrangements

Living situation, own or rent, members of household

Travel, moving, or transportation arrangements

Race, Religion, Gender, Citizenship, Nationality

Race

Family cultural background, country of origin, citizenry, birthplace

Name of place of worship, religious holidays

Sexual preference

Views about sexual preference, race, nationalities, etc.

Memberships in social, religious, community, political groups

Hobbies

Personal Health

Age, birth date

Height, weight

Recent or past illnesses, operations

Date of last physical exam

Family's health

Status of eyesight, physical well-being

Finances

Financial situation, debts, sources of income, banking information

Bankruptcy, credit rating

Criminal Record

Arrests

Convictions unrelated to the job

(Questions related to criminal record may vary by state and should be checked with the legal representation of the organization)

Military

Type of discharge

The Americans with Disabilities Act provides detailed information about appropriate questions and interview strategies. Under this act, an employer may ask disability-related questions and require medical examinations of an applicant only after the applicant has been given a conditional job offer. Reasons for rejection of a candidate with a disability must be "job-related and consistent with business necessity" or because of a "direct threat" to the safety of the candidate or others, that cannot be reduced through reasonable accommodation. Note that the Americans with Disabilities Act provides guidelines on "self-identity" of candidates.

Do Not Ask About:

- existence of a disability
- nature, name of disability
- level of severity
- mental health history, current mental health diagnoses
- the necessity of reasonable accommodations (such as parking space, adapted work station, elevator, etc.) to perform the job–unless the employer reasonably believes that accommodation will be needed because of an obvious disability, or because a disability was revealed by the candidate that might affect job function

- status of an impairment (e.g., broken leg)
- major life activities (e.g., walking, standing) unless necessary to perform the job
- workers' compensation history
- medications, treatments, past prescriptions (unless results of lawful drug use will be revealed in a drug test)
- quantity and/or frequency of past illegal drug use, including alcohol
- treatment for illegal drug use, including alcohol.

It is advisable that interviewers become familiar with the contents of the Americans with Disabilities Act, making sure that the interviewers are up-to-date about recent legal decisions. If interviewers are concerned about asking the right questions and taking the proper approach to interviews, ask a Human Resources/Personnel representative to assist with preinterview planning or to sit in on the interview.

Always keep in mind that candidates are more than likely aware of the requirements of a job and have made the personal decision that they can handle the job responsibilities. A pregnant candidate has undoubtedly considered the physical demands of a job, a man over 50 is well aware of his age, and a female candidate has undoubtedly made a choice about working in a male-dominated field. Find out if the candidates *meet the requirements* by asking questions that are *job-related.* For example:

- Are you able to perform essential functions of the job with or without reasonable accommodation?
- Ask after full explanation of the job has been given.
- Ask if the disability is obvious.
- Ask if a candidate has volunteered information about the disability.
- Ask if a candidate has volunteered information about the need for accommodation.
- Ask if there is reasonable belief that a candidate will need accommodation.
  If yes: what type of accommodation would you need?
- Describe or demonstrate how you would perform job tasks.
  Ask everyone or not at all.

- Ask if directly tied to ability to carry out the job functions even with accommodations.
- Do not ask: What was your past attendance record?
  Ask: Can you meet our attendance requirements?

In some cases, permission to gather further information may be granted by the finalists, such as questions about race, relocation, credit rating, and other characteristics that pertain to affirmative action, job success, or organizational requirements. Check with the legal department of the organization before asking the questions, even if permission has been granted voluntarily.

If an illegal question is asked, candidates can:

- Answer the question.
- Refuse to answer the question.
- Examine the intent of the question and give a job-related response.
- Point out that the question is not allowed to be asked.
- Volunteer information up front.

It is the candidate's right to refuse to answer. Do not discount candidates if they make that choice.

8. WHAT QUESTIONS CAN BE ASKED?

Interviewers are often concerned that they will inadvertently ask a question that is biased or illegal. As a result, they tend to stay clear of questions that appear to be personal, but at some point need to be asked. The following questions are generally safe to ask, as long as the wording is not changed. Again, check with Human Resources/ Personnel and legal representatives to confirm the use of the questions. Make sure that the question is job-related and must be asked to determine if the candidate's skills and experiences match the job.

Go Ahead And Ask:

- Do you have any responsibilities that conflict with job attendance or travel?

- Are you available for weekend work?
- What is your address?
- Is the location of the job a problem?
- Can you provide proof of your eligibility to work in the United States?
- Are you fluent in any languages other than English? (Ask if job-related.)
- What is your Social Security number?
- Would you be willing to relocate if necessary?
- Would you be able to provide proof that you are over the age of 18?
- Would you be able to work overtime if necessary? (Ask if job-related.)
- Are you able to (carry, lift, push, etc.) as required by the job?
- Have you ever been convicted of a crime? (Crime must be directly job-related, such as embezzlement)?
- In what branch of the military did you serve?
- What type of training or education have you received?
- Have you belonged to job-related professional organizations or trade groups?
- Where have you worked before and what were your responsibilities?
- What special qualifications do you have for this job?
- What certifications and licenses do you have?

9. WHAT QUESTIONS DO CANDIDATES EXPECT?

Although it is tempting to create interview questions that are unique, some standard interview questions should be asked. The candidate has probably prepared answers to routine questions and can get comfortable if the basic questions are asked at the beginning of the interview. They can be considered "warm-up" questions, but can still provide valuable information.

The order of the questions depends upon the type of interview, but it is best to start out with general topics and then hone in on specific skill areas. On some occasions, initial responses will reveal how long the interview should continue.

Questions That Candidates Prepare For:

- Why did you apply for this position?
- What are your strengths?
- How can you improve?
- How are you qualified for this job?
- What have you read lately?
- Tell us about yourself.
- What aspects of your current position do you like/dislike?
- What do you see yourself doing five years from now?
- What qualifications do you have that would make you successful here?
- What are the qualities of a good (employee, manager, team member, customer service representative, etc.)?
- Why did you leave your job/consider looking for a new job?

Questions That Candidates May Have Thought About:

- What are your finest accomplishments at work?
- Why are you pursuing this job in particular?
- What is appealing to you about this job?
- What concerns do you have about this job?
- What rewards are important to you?
- How could you use your skills in this job?
- What supervisory/teamwork/travel/training experience have you had?
- What skill areas would you like to develop?
- How do you think your background ties to the job requirements?

10. WHAT QUESTIONS MAY NOT BE EXPECTED?

It is important to begin the interview with standard questions that the candidates may expect, to put the candidates at ease. More challenging questions should be introduced later, when the candidates are more comfortable. It is essential that the question be asked without elaboration or suggested responses. Listen carefully to the answers as the candidates react to the questions, weigh their responses, and choose what to say.

Questions That Candidates May Not Expect:

- What drives you crazy at work?
- How can you help to make this a job of your dreams?
- What do you think that you do particularly well?
- How have you turned weaknesses into strengths?
- How would you define (choose a job-related term)?
- What are some things that you would like to avoid in a job?
- When are you the most productive at work?
- What are examples of how you communicate with colleagues?
- When do you feel the most confident?
- When should you have been recognized by your boss?
- When do you think teamwork is unsuccessful?
- How do your career goals relate to those you had 5-10 years ago?
- What have you learned from your mistakes?
- How would you handle. . . ?
- What would you do if. . . ?

Once interviewers have determined the qualities they are looking for in candidates, it is a good idea to create open-ended questions that may reveal those qualities. Below are qualities that may be of interest to the organization, followed by questions that may bring out information about those qualities:

Relationship To Authority

- Who was the best boss/teacher you ever had?
- How did you handle disagreements with a former boss or teacher?

Record Of Success

- What was an accomplishment at work/school, big or small?
- When were you the most successful in school/training?

Reaction To Pressure

- What do you do when you know you are right and others disagree?

- What deadlines have you met?
- What jobs have you had that involved "busy" and "slow" periods of work?
- How do you get ready for an approaching deadline?
- How do you handle several tasks at the same time?

Reactions To Change

- Do you think that things change too much at work?
- How have you changed something that you thought needed improving?

Rational Thought Process

- What if. . .
- Suppose. . .

(Give a hypothetical work-related problem.)

Self-Knowledge

- What would you most like to improve about yourself at work?
- What have we missed covering in this interview?
- How will you go about achieving your goals?
- What do you think will be interesting about this job?

Basic Employability Skills

- Why is it important to be on time for work?
- What would you do if you were having difficulty with a task at work?
- Is the customer always right?
- What is the most difficult problem that you solved at work?
- If you could spend the day on one work task, what would it be?
- What training do you wish you had completed?
- What if you do not know the answer to something?

Interviewers should combine basic background questions with open-ended questions that are unexpected but essential for determining the most qualified candidate.

11. WHAT ARE THE SIX RULES OF INTERVIEWING?

Details for each of the rules described in this section can be found throughout the other sections, but these basic rules should be kept in mind throughout the entire interview process:

RULE 1. *Know the most important qualities that you must see.*

Determine ahead of time what you are looking for and discuss those qualities with your cointerviewers. Identify qualities that are essential for the position.

Sample *essential* qualities are:

- enthusiasm for the work
- communication skills
- rational thought process
- work ethic
- problem-solving ability
- planning and organization
- willingness to grow and learn
- reactions to pressure and change.

Discuss how to ask the right questions to determine if the candidates have the qualities that you seek.

RULE 2: *Ask yourself why you are asking.*

After the interviewers list the questions that they would like to ask the candidates, the most important step is to rule out questions that are biased or illegal. Every question should be designed to gather essential job-related information.

Set aside preconceived notions. Make sure that questions are not based on conclusions related to attributes such as the candidate's accent, choice of jewelry, hairstyle, and so forth.

- Ask yourself: Do your questions reveal your *assumptions?*
- Watch for small talk made by the interviewer that could imply bias or an attempt to indirectly gather biased information (or information that cannot be gathered legally), such as comments like:

Did you have a long drive?

At your age you don't need bifocals like mine.

We are investigating putting a ramp on the other side of the building.

Didn't I see you at _____?

RULE 3: *Do not guess–do not assume–find out.*

If you have heard something about the candidate, ask questions to get a true picture. Do not rely on gossip.

If the question was never answered by the candidate, ask it again. Do not assume that they were avoiding the question or did not know the answer. There is no point in commenting after the interview that the question was never answered. Pursue the question!

Use the interview to get further information, especially if an answer is confusing or uninformative. You should not be guessing later about the meaning of a response. Ask for clarification. Start sentences with:

- I'm confused. . .
- Help me to understand something. . .
- Can you explain again. . .
- Please clarify something for me. . .

Can you call a candidate after the interview to get further clarification? Yes. Take notes.

RULE 4: *Combine records, explanations, words, and facts.*

All information pertaining to the candidate should be available during the interview. Have applications and resumes handy. Make sure that they have been reviewed and highlighted before the interview.

Give opportunities for the candidate to elaborate on the paperwork by raising questions and highlighting areas that need further clarification.

Listen closely to words and phrases, watching body language. Examples:

- "assisted" versus "directed"
- "learned" versus "completed training"

- "frustrated" versus "angry"
- "involved" versus "organized"
- "easily bored" versus "anxious to try new things."

Sometimes the phraseology is a poor choice of words, so ask the candidates what they meant to say. Wording can be quite revealing!

RULE 5: Be hypercritical, yet fair.

An interview is the time to be cordial and professional, maintaining objectivity and an open mind. Be alert to problems, keeping in mind that the interviewers might be working with the new hire for a very long time.

If the behavior of the candidates seems odd, or skills obviously need development, or the answers are vague, it may be:

- the tension of the interview
- attempts to mask information or to avoid providing details
- personal bias on the part of the interviewer
- poor questions
- a poor candidate.

Frame questions so that the candidates have opportunities to overcome anxiety, and can comfortably reveal information about themselves. Remember that some of the best candidates are unaccustomed to talking about themselves. In fact, they may see it as bragging and are, therefore, not very forthcoming. Explain that the questions will be pursued if the interviewers need more information in order to form an accurate picture of the qualifications of the candidates.

If you are hypercritical and the candidates still look pretty good, then the choice is easier to make. Do not gloss over any basic weaknesses because you liked the candidates personally.

Do not eliminate candidates because their style or interests are different than yours. (At the same time, do not hire someone just because they have the same hobbies or interests!)

Base evaluations on facts. In hindsight, you should be able to reflect that you were critiquing fairly throughout the interview.

RULE 6: Gain confirmation of your evaluation.

It is best to compile notes immediately after the interview *without talking to cointerviewers or other coworkers.* It is hard, however, to refrain from commenting about candidates, especially if the interviews were particularly unusual.

Discussing the interview in general terms is inevitable, but keep an open mind, check over notes, and be prepared to change opinions later. Initial reactions will be hard to ignore, but the purpose of a later discussion is to share reactions. Interviewers may have been misreading a situation, or may have noticed something that others missed. When reviewing all of the candidates together, it is easier to compare and conclude.

Interviewers will not always agree. If uncertain about final selections, make sure a protocol has been established for follow-up interviews, especially if final candidates may be invited to meet with senior management.

Good notes will help to keep candidates from becoming a blurred memory. Use notes as a reference for discussing each candidate individually, and for creating a ranking of finalists.

12. WHEN SHOULD AN INTERVIEW BE ENDED?

Sometimes it is readily apparent in an interview that a candidate is not right for the job. Discuss before the interview who can end an interview, how the interview will be terminated, on what basis it will end, and what will be the signal that the interview should end. (In some cases, it is obvious to both the candidate and the interviewers that pursuing the interview is not appropriate, and the interviewers can be clear and direct about ending the interview.) Interviewers who wish to be more indirect may signal by moving a pencil, asking a prearranged question, or using some other subtle signal to alert colleagues that the interview should be concluded. Discussion prior to the interview will limit confusion should the occasion arise.

Responses from a candidate may show that the candidate:

- is not interested
- is clearly not qualified

• is demonstrating inappropriate behavior
• has questionable credentials.

There is no point in wasting everyone's time if it is very clear that the candidate will not be considered for the job.

For example, here are actual quotes that have ended an interview:

"I can't be here to answer phones that early."
"As soon as my boyfriend finishes law school I'm out of here."
"Everyone says that this is a cushy job."
"I have an RV and prefer to take August off for vacation."
"I like to do things one at a time."
"I've had personality conflicts with my bosses. They don't understand me."
"I hate working under pressure."
"My life is a mess."

It is also important to plan the strategy for calling another interviewer *into* or *out of* an interview. Determine if a planned interruption is necessary, and how to handle the rest of the interview. It is a good idea to have a colleague on call should a second opinion be needed about ending the interview.

13. HOW CAN TELEPHONE INTERVIEWS BE CONDUCTED?

Interviews may have to be conducted on the phone for out-of-town candidates or for screening several applicants. Although it is better to interview potential employees in person, phone interviews can be quite revealing. They can allow the interviewers to concentrate on the communication style and the content of the answers of the candidates, rather than on appearance and mannerisms. Phone interviews, if conducted well, can force the interviewers to listen more closely to what the candidates are saying, especially if the interviewers refrain from interrupting!

After the phone interview, if it appears that a candidate may be appropriate for the job, every effort should be made to arrange for the candidate to visit the organization. This not only gives the future employer a chance to interact with the candidate personally, but also provides the candidate an opportunity to assess the working environment.

Some tips to effective phone interviews follow:

Set It Up

The strategies for an effective phone interview are similar to an onsite interview. The same preparations should take place and the same rules apply for asking appropriate and legal questions.

Make sure that the candidates know:

• who places the call
• who will be participating in the interview
• what paperwork will be expected to be handy
• the time frame of the interview
• the need for an uninterrupted phone call.

Conduct the interviews in a quiet, private place, making sure that there will be no interruptions or background noise. Arrange questions ahead of time, and have all paperwork handy. If it is an interview involving a speakerphone or a teleconference, test the equipment before the interview, and arrange furniture so that all interviewers and the candidate can be heard. If there are multiple interviewers, discuss the procedures so that everyone knows who will facilitate the interview, who will do the overview of the organization and the job, and in what order the questions will be asked. Remind interviewers that they must give the candidate time to respond to their questions. During phone interviews, there is a tendency for some interviewers to ask long questions and attempt to carry on a conversation with the candidate. Interviewers need to ask their question and then *wait*.

Sometimes candidates cannot help it if a phone call is interrupted by a doorbell, crying child, siren, or other background noise. Do not try to continue the conversation if the candidates will clearly be distracted. Offer to call back in a few minutes, expressing understanding that sometimes "unanticipated events" interfere with the interview process.

Explain The Format

Just as in an on-site interview, explain the format of the interview to the candidates. Give the general organization of the interview, assuring the candidates that the process will be the same as that used for on-site interviews.

One of the most difficult aspects of phone interviews is that the candidates cannot read body language to determine if the listeners (the interviewers) are comprehending their responses. However, if the interviewers keep verbalizing their responses ("Yes," "uh-huh," "true," etc.), then it can be confusing for the speaker and can interrupt train of thought. Let the candidates know that silence at the other end of the line does not mean that everyone has fallen asleep. If there is silence, then it means that the interviewers are listening and will follow up with more questions for clarification.

The beauty of phone interviews is that candidates tend to want to fill the silence. They talk more. Interviewers learn more if they sit quietly and listen.

Take Notes

One of the advantages of phone interviews is that the listeners can take more extensive notes. Be careful not to write down personal impressions, but do focus on whether the responses of the candidates seem to match the job requirements. Write down actual quotes and information provided, not guesses about appearance or personal reactions to the candidates.

Establish Rapport

After explaining the format of the phone interview, explain to the candidates that meeting them in person would be preferable, but the purpose of the phone contact is to gather information. Point out that the interviewers all have background material in front of them for use as a reference. Describe the setting, such as a conference room or office. Ask each of the interviewers to say hello and to give one sentence about their role in the organization. Remember that the candidates have to imagine the participants. There is no need to provide detailed descriptions of the roles and responsibilities of each interviewer, but it helps if the candidates can try to envision the setting.

To make the candidates feel more at ease, begin with basic background questions that confirm the contents of a resume or application. (Make sure that the questions have been approved by Human Resources/Personnel or legal representatives.) Give the candidates the chance to become comfortable talking on the phone to people the candidates have probably never met.

Watch For Nerves

Nervousness on the part of the candidates will show up differently during phone interviews. Some candidates are unfamiliar with using the phone for extended conversations and interviews, and will think that they need to shout into the phone if there is a speakerphone, or will answer with monosyllabic responses. (If they are chewing gum or breathing directly into the phone, mention that it "sounds like" gum or breathing and it is hard to hear.) Encourage the candidates to answer the questions just as they would in an on-site interview. If they seem to need to be drawn out, explain that each question is designed so that specifics can be provided in the answers. Tell them not to hesitate to provide details, even if they feel that the answers are contained in the written application materials.

Occasionally, a phone candidate rambles on, talking too much. Explain that there are several questions, each one requiring a four- to five- sentence response. If the candidate still cannot keep from providing lengthy answers, determine whether the style will matter in fulfilling the job responsibilities. It may be necessary to end the interview.

Screen First

If the purpose of the phone interview is to screen applicants for future on-site interviews, then ask crucial questions right away. Although explaining the format and establishing rapport is still important, a lot of time can be saved if elimination questions are asked immediately. Check on required degrees and certifications, years of experience, and so forth. Verify information provided in application materials.

Be careful not to draw conclusions about the candidates on the basis of tone, accent, colloquialisms, grammar, and other voice and language factors. If the job requirements are very specific about communication skills (especially on the phone), then these factors may be viewed as determinants for further interviewing. Interviewers should ask themselves as they are listening to the candidates:

- Will the accent (tenor, speech pattern, etc.) affect ability to do the job tasks?
- Could training and experience improve possible communication problems?
- Are conclusions being drawn on the basis of stereotypes and prejudice?

If it is difficult to determine if the communication style is a hindrance, it may be necessary to invite the applicant in for an on-site interview.

Allow For Questions

Candidates who are interviewed on the phone are at a disadvantage because they cannot see the organization firsthand. Even if marketing materials or websites are available to candidates, it is important to provide more detailed information about the working environment.

After the general background information has been provided, and questions have been covered, it may be necessary to provide specifics about the organization, such as:

- environmental setting and access
- grounds, parking
- size of building(s), number of employees
- working environment for the job
- access to cafeterias, local shopping, etc.

Even if candidates are going to be invited on-site for a second interview, they should be provided details so that they have the opportunity to decide whether the job still sounds appealing.

Allow extra time for phone candidates to ask questions about the organization since they will not be able to witness things for themselves.

14. WHAT SHOULD BE DONE AFTER THE INTERVIEW?

After each interview it is tempting to immediately start analyzing candidates once they have left the interview room or hung up the phone. If they are especially unusual candidates, it is inevitable that their behaviors will be discussed. A few initial reactions will probably occur, but interviewers can conduct a quick and professional postinterview conference if they discuss the following points for each candidate:

• general overall reaction
• high points of the interview
• concerns about the interview
• assessment of the interview process and fairness to the candidate.

If it is determined that the candidate should still be considered, then organize personal notes for a more in-depth discussion later. Refrain from discussing details, as the conversation will influence the ability to take a fresh view of upcoming candidates. Notes should be clear and accurate so that they are useful when all candidates are reviewed.

Once all interviews have been conducted, the interviewers should meet to compare observations. Single interviewers may want to rank choices, review notes to support the ranking, and arrange for follow-up interviews to verify impressions.

Discuss the criteria for selection and match the job requirements to each candidate. This sounds easy, but it can be confusing if a candidate was impressive but not completely qualified, or if a candidate has potential but obvious areas of skill deficits. If the final selections are not completely clear (or there is disagreement), it only makes sense to conduct second interviews. Keep following up to find out more.

Remember: once someone is hired, they will cost the organization money. Aside from salary and benefits, there may be relocation costs, training expenses, and perhaps even the cost of coaching, counseling, termination, and rehiring (if a poor selection was made).

Take the time to get to know candidates and to help them become familiar with the organization. After all, they, too, are forming impressions. Organize a personal tour, introduce the candidate to senior management for a follow-up interview, give the candidate time with potential coworkers, conduct team meetings, and set up on-the-job time for the candidate to observe and demonstrate work skills. If possible, conduct necessary skill-related tests and surveys.

The investment in time for finalists will help to weed out candidates who glow during the interview and fade afterward. Or the postinterview activities may reveal that a candidate is an outstanding worker, but just cannot express those skills very well in an interview or on an application or resume.

Always, always, always check references and verify credentials. The Human Resources/Personnel Department should carry out this process, if possible. Prepare questions ahead of time so that further information about the candidate can be gathered. (Check with the Human Resources/Personnel or legal representation of the organization to make sure that the questions are appropriate and legal.)

Keep in mind that in some cases candidates can be very impressive in an interview, but they have exaggerated or lied about their background. Even the best interviewers can be fooled. Gather together *all* information on the candidate, and check it all out, to feel confident that thorough research has been done.

Some businesses will only offer verification of employment or refuse to offer detailed information about why an employee is leaving a job. Some candidates would prefer that former (or current) employers not be contacted. Respect these requests, adding the information to all of the data gathered.

If the interview questions were presented for the purpose of finding out details and clarifying information, then the interviewers should be satisfied that they have a complete picture. The picture may still look good, or the final picture may cause just enough concern to cause the candidate to be rejected. If interviewers feel that they have adequately prepared for the interviews, conducted thoughtful and fair interviews, and have carried out thorough postinterview activities, then they have done their best to identify who should be hired.

15. IS THE SELECTION OF A FINALIST ALWAYS FAIR?

Selection of finalists will not always seem fair because of the influences of office politics, contract restrictions, unions, friendships, leadership preferences, the job market, and so forth.

Even when they are aware that outside factors may influence the final decision, interviewers should feel confident that proper interviewing steps were taken, and they are able to say "yes" to the question:

Were the interviews fair?

Human Resources/Personnel or legal representation of the organization need to be involved if there are concerns about bias or discrimination.

16. WHAT SHOULD BE DONE AFTER THE SELECTION OF A FINALIST?

The hiring of an applicant does not conclude with the interview. It is important to follow up the process by verifying what was read in the paperwork and heard in the interview.

- Verify college attendance, training programs, certifications.
- Determine how reference checks can be conducted, and *check them.*
- Take notes as a record of verification.
- Confirm training and other benefits offered to the finalist.
- Review organizational policies about conducting job offers.
- Notify candidates who have not been selected.
- Follow organizational protocols for orienting new employees and informing coworkers about new hires.

Occasionally candidates who do *not* receive a job offer will ask why they were rejected. Although it may be tempting to provide helpful advice, even a hint at areas of improvement or deficits could result in a rejected candidate researching the background of the new hire and questioning whether the final selection was fair. Interviewers should feel confident that they followed the steps to ensure a fair interview but should not reveal any information about the hiring process.

Chapter 4

THE TRUTH ABOUT PERFORMANCE APPRAISALS

I'm way, way behind in doing performance appraisals.
(Financial Services Supervisor, looking at her full calendar.)

When supervisors are asked how they feel about performance appraisals, they respond with a groan. They often see them as time-consuming, stressful, and another obligation that requires paperwork. They fret about what to write and what to say, and they often fall behind in getting the appraisal forms done on time. Many supervisors feel that the appraisal process is discomforting, the forms are cumbersome, and the results are uninformative.

Yet employees do need to be evaluated. They have a right to know how they are doing, and, in some cases, they need a formal appraisal to determine salaries and bonuses. Employees also need direction and guidance from their supervisors, and the chance to articulate personal goals and interests.

Supervisors need the opportunity to strategically review the expectations of the organizational leadership, and the accomplishments of employees. They can use a formal appraisal meeting for supporting and encouraging employees, as well as for helping them to modify work behaviors.

By establishing a standardized performance appraisal system, organizations are providing a structured opportunity to review accomplishments and set goals for the future. If the appraisal system is tailored to the organization and designed for efficiency, it can be beneficial to both the supervisors and the employees.

This chapter provides practical information on how to design and implement a system that is useful and comfortable, so that even supervisors look forward to performance appraisals.

1. WHAT IS A PERFORMANCE APPRAISAL?

A performance appraisal consists of a written summary of an employee's work performance in the past, as well as plans for work behaviors in the future. Sometimes referred to as a performance "review" or "evaluation," the performance appraisal gives supervisors a chance to formally record the achievements of employees. It also covers the areas that need further development and improvement, and the goals for the months ahead. Using a standardized format, usually an evaluation form tailored to the organization, supervisors rate work competencies and behaviors of employees. In some cases, narrative comments are also included on the form, or the entire appraisal is narrative.

The completed appraisal forms are discussed with employees during performance appraisal meetings. (Employees may also have the opportunity to self-assess prior to their meetings so that the supervisor and employees can compare observations.) The meetings are a chance to review the appraisals in detail, with the supervisor and employees exchanging information and setting goals together. A final appraisal form is completed, signed by both parties (if required by the organization), and added to the personnel file of the employees. Most appraisals are carried out annually on the anniversary date of hire, but some organizations prefer to conduct them at the beginning of a new year or more frequently during the year.

The term *performance appraisal* has become popular because the *value* of an employee is being appraised during the evaluation process. How has the employee contributed to achieving organizational goals? How much investment (e.g., training, promotions, raises) should be dedicated to the employee? Is the employee an asset to the organization? Regardless of the terminology, the appraisal is designed to encourage supervisors to take the time to let employees know how well they are doing on the job and what is expected from them in the future.

The performance appraisal process can be very rewarding, but it can also be time-consuming and stressful, especially if communication between the supervisor and employees has not been taking place on a regular basis. The deadline for the appraisal may suddenly loom and supervisors may feel unprepared. Supervisors may resist the paperwork or may avoid an appraisal meeting that could be uncomfortable. In some cases, supervisors may be concerned that a poor appraisal of an employee reflects negatively on the leadership of the supervisor.

Employees may have mixed emotions because they want to know the supervisor's view of their work, but they may not want to hear about skill areas that need improvement. If the appraisal determines salary increments and bonuses, then employees are usually anxious to hear the "bottom line" of the appraisal.

In other words, both supervisors and employees usually approach performance appraisals with ambivalence. It is not always easy to openly discuss the work performance of employees and the income that they will be receiving. It is not always easy to hear the observations of the supervisor. But the appraisal process can clarify goals and expectations, can provide praise and encouragement, and can be used to identify contributions and personal objectives of the employees. If it is the culmination of ongoing feedback from supervisors and results in better communication between supervisors and employees, then the formal appraisal experience is well worth the time.

(See Chapter 5 for information on 360° performance appraisals.)

2. WHY ARE PERFORMANCE APPRAISALS NECESSARY?

Performance appraisals serve many purposes. Even though supervisors may groan when an appraisal is due, the benefits of conducting the appraisal process become apparent as the appraisals are completed. Appraisals are necessary because they:

Provide Feedback On A One-To-One Basis

The appraisal meeting allows employees to receive the undivided attention of the supervisor. It gives employees the opportunity to discuss goals and aspirations, to obtain support and approval for new activities, and to receive vital assessments of progress and achievements. It can also inform employees about their role in the overall mission of the organization, reinforcing the value of individual contributions. Hopefully, ongoing communication and coaching have already encouraged discussion of these topics, but the appraisal process can formalize agreements.

Document Accomplishments

The written appraisal can provide a formal summary of the achievements of employees. In many organizations, the performance appraisal is stored permanently in the personnel files.

Encourage Behaviors

Appraisals can reinforce positive work behaviors and can outline desirable behaviors for the future. They can encourage employees to learn, try new skill areas, and expand horizons, thereby maximizing their contribution to the organization and building the confidence of employees.

Discourage Behaviors

Appraisals can specify behaviors that need to be improved or changed.

Reduce Uncertainty

Even if supervisors have been providing continuous feedback to employees, it is reassuring to see evaluations in writing. The appraisals may not always be completely positive, but the employees do not have to depend on guessing or on their personal interpretation of verbal feedback.

The appraisal process is a joint effort. The written appraisal provides a mutual agreement that clearly states what is expected. Early appraisals for new employees, such as after the first six months on the job, can reduce uncertainty about progress and job status.

Establish Standards

During the appraisal process information can be provided about how work behaviors will be measured and what standards are expected to be met. Supposedly employees have already been informed about organizational standards, but the appraisal meeting can be a good opportunity to clarify and reinforce.

Save Money

Staff turnover is expensive. It can cost the organization time and money to counsel, discipline, and terminate employees, and then to rehire. Continuous feedback and coaching are essential, with a formal appraisal to track performance and retain employees.

Provide Reward And Recognition

It is often during the appraisal process that supervisors have to make decisions about monetary increments and rewards, promotions, public recognition, and selection of employees for special projects and awards. The entire appraisal process encourages supervisors to gather data to support decisions, and to share observations and praise with employees and coworkers.

Provide Organizational Information

The results of performance appraisals will reveal valuable information to the organization such as the impact of training programs, skill areas that need attention, and hierarchical changes that may be necessary. The results can be used to design progression plans and new organizational goals. The appraisal results will also show whether the organization's process of evaluation yields useful results.

Build Relationships

If performance appraisals are carried out effectively, then supervisors have worked *with* employees to identify strengths and goals. Communication flows so that supervisors feel that they have been able to convey observations and expectations. Employees feel that their needs and concerns were taken seriously, and that they are clear about their personal value to the organization. The chance to stop and assess can facilitate teamwork and strong relationships between employees and their supervisors.

3. WHAT SHOULD APPRAISAL FORMS LOOK LIKE?

There are hundreds of different types of performance appraisal forms. Some are strictly scales for rating skills, some are narrative format, some are a mixture of numerical scores and comments, and some are based on formulas and percentages that measure behaviors and accomplishments. The length of the forms may vary from a short one-page checklist to pages of detailed questions.

The format and contents of the appraisal will depend upon the goals of the organization. The following factors should be taken into consideration when determining what the appraisal form should look like:

Time

It is essential that supervisors complete appraisal forms in a timely manner. The length and complexity of the form, as well as the information that must be compiled to conduct the appraisal, will determine how long each appraisal will take to complete. Sometimes organizations get so involved in creating detailed forms that the time factor gets lost.

Calculate how long performance appraisals, including meetings, will actually take the supervisors. How many employees are they supervising? How long does the form take to complete for each employee? How long will each appraisal meeting take? All total, how many hours will supervisors realistically spend on performance appraisals? Does the form need to be more efficient and compact so that supervisors can complete them on time and give them the attention that they deserve?

Timing

Performance appraisals are usually conducted annually. The date of review may be determined by the hiring anniversary date or by a set time period, such as the beginning of a new year, the end of an academic year, or at the conclusion of a busy season.

The forms should be designed to reflect the time of the appraisal. If employees are evaluated after the implementation of a major annual conference, then questions specifically related to the conference should be included. If the organization traditionally faces a seasonal workload, the form should reflect the skills that are needed to respond to the changes in work patterns.

It only makes sense to time the deadlines of performance appraisals when supervisors are going to be able to get them completed. Although supervisors are generally busy all year long, they should not be required to conduct appraisals when it is known that the workload will be particularly demanding.

The appraisal forms should be designed to reflect the timing of the fiscal year, if they are connected to raises and bonuses

Some organizations require an "interim appraisal" to be discussed midyear. The purpose of the discussion is to determine if the supervisor and employees have the same perceptions of progress and goal achievement. Results are usually not formalized in a written document.

Contents

Performance appraisals should measure exactly what the organization wants to know about employees. Sometimes an off-the-shelf form is used that assesses work behaviors that are not relevant to the organization or the profession. For example, "public speaking" or "customer service" may not apply. Select skills for the form that are based on the organization, the job, and expectations related to the job. Be *specific.*

Vague:	Effective customer service
Specific:	Treats all customers with respect
	Greets customers professionally
	Follows through on customer requests
Vague:	Communicates well with coworkers
Specific:	Communicates on a regular basis with supervisors
	Gives clear directions
	Informs coworkers about daily work and goals

It may be necessary to tailor the contents according to the profession and required tasks. Accounting skills and marketing skills may overlap in some areas (time and attendance, knowledge of new techniques, working on a team, etc.), but they will be very different in other areas. It is important to give employees the chance to be measured on what they are actually expected to do. Combine the generally expected skills for all employees with the profession-related skills.

Rating

The fastest format of an appraisal form is a rating system, allowing supervisors to give employees a "score" for each skill area. Rating can be quick and efficient, but employees should not just be handed a "report card" and the appraisal is over. Rating systems should be clear and informative, and the written form should always be discussed in an appraisal meeting.

Most supervisors are familiar with rating, but may become frustrated if the range is too broad. It is recommended that supervisors be able to choose a score of either a "1," "2," "3," or "4" for each skill level. If the range is 1-5, then supervisors can easily choose the "3" in the middle if they are undecided, unfamiliar with the work, or uncertain about how to rate the employee. By limiting supervisors to four choices, they are forced to make a clear decision. A "1" usually means that the employee is very weak in the skill area and needs training, coaching, or even discipline. A "2" indicates that the skill is not a strong point and assistance may be required (or more attention on the part of the employee may be required). A "3" indicates very satisfactory work, and a "4" usually implies exceptional work that is consistently outstanding. For example:

```
1 = unsatisfactory
2 = improvement required
3 = excellent work
4 = consistent exceptional work
```

or

```
1 = unacceptable
2 = progressing
3 = fully meets requirements
4 = exceeds requirements
```

It is essential that all supervisors are able to interpret the numbers in the same fashion. The organization can attach descriptions to each number, going beyond "Excellent," "Good," "Fair," and "Poor." How does an employee earn a "3" or "4"? What would it take to receive a "1" during a performance appraisal? Provide a description for each number that all supervisors can use as a guide. For example:

Example #1

> 1 Performance sporadic or no results are accomplished
> Fails to meet job requirements
> Does not demonstrate expected behaviors
>
> 2 Occasionally meets expectations
> Needs improvement in quality, quantity, speed, and/or accuracy
> Working to build skills
>
> 3 Performance is fully effective in accomplishing results
> Consistently meets job requirements
> Occasionally exceeds expected behaviors
>
> 4 Regularly exceeds expectations
> Consistently superior performance
> Demonstrated mastery of job requirements
> Recognized by coworkers as an expert resource

Example #2

> Customer Service
>
> 1 Customer complaints, poor treatment of customers, poor follow-through
>
> 2 Inconsistent treatment of customers and follow-through
>
> 3 Pleasant, solves problems, follows through
>
> 4 Consistently pleasant, solves problems, sells new products, follows through, maintains repeat customers, cultivates new customers

Some supervisors hesitate to give even their best employees the highest score because "no one is perfect." If the scores are clearly described, there may be employees who do exceptionally well in all of the skill areas. Supervisors should understand that outstanding employees generally work to maintain their high ratings, and should be rewarded for fine work by receiving high scores.

Ranking

Employees should not be ranked (top to bottom) or even compared when the performance appraisals are being completed. Each employee is measured independently. The form should be designed so that each question can be answered specifically for the individual being evaluated.

Having said that, it is inevitable that supervisors may do some mental comparisons. They may think:

"How does Mary measure up to Jackie, who is clearly my best employee?"

"How does Tom compare to José when meeting with customers? José's closure record is the highest of the team. Do I rate Tom lower because José is clearly superior? Or do I rate Tom with a high score because he is not as experienced and doing his best?"

Mary, Jackie, Tom, and José should not be measured against each other, but measured by the standards that are specified on the form. If the descriptions of each skill and each rating score on the assessment are very clear, then it is easier to evaluate without comparing. For example, if the standards for customer service are known to everyone, then Tom can be compared to the standard, rather than to José.

Ranking may occur when raises and bonuses are connected to the performance appraisal results. If ratings are totaled for a final score, a ranked list may be established. Some organizations devise formulas for supervisor reference for determining the increment allotted for each total score (e.g., a total score of 60 = 4% raise). Others calculate how to divide up the budgeted money once the scores have been compiled and ranked.

Needless to say, if it is necessary to create a ranked list, it should not be posted or released to employees.

Skills

There are basic work skills that are usually included in all performance appraisal forms. Additional skills can be added as they pertain to specific job titles and responsibilities. The following chart shows basic skills (also referred to as "behaviors" and "competencies") that might be included on the forms. Specific details can be added as the organization determines what is required.

WORK ETHIC	*JOB KNOWLEDGE*	*ORGANIZATION*
• attendance • follows policies and procedures • punctual • professional • goal-oriented • meets deadlines	• command of basic skills • task completion • pursues knowledge • pursues skill enhancement • cost-effective • safety practices	• plans • prioritizes • efficient • coordinates activities • delegates • maintains work area • accurate records
COMMUNICATION	*PRODUCTIVITY*	*TEAMWORK*
• clear, articulate (verbal and written) • clear directions • promotes business • addresses problems professionally • public speaking • coaches/mentors • inter-shift communication	• maintains pace • time-on-task • produces quantity required • maintains quality • meets quotas/standards • continuous improvement	• dependable • provides information and support • consults with team • cross-trains • resolves conflicts • supports goals
CUSTOMER SERVICE	*INITIATIVE*	*PROBLEM-SOLVING*
• greets positively • follows through • solves customer problems • cultivates new clients • maintains client base	• takes on leadership • strives for improvements • seeks new knowledge • pursues new tasks • preventive maintenance	• tackles problems • creative solutions • systematic approach • cost-effective solutions • synthesizes data to solve problems

Comments

Room for comments should be included on performance appraisal forms, but not as a "general comments" section. General comments can be hard to write, and supervisors often end up writing variations of the same remarks. Supervisors should be able to write comments *for each skill area*, if they feel comments are necessary.

The purpose of the comments should be to explain why a particular rating was selected. For example, if a supervisor gives an employee the highest score possible on a particular skill area, then it is helpful to elaborate. What behaviors impressed the supervisor the most? What can the employee keep doing to maintain the high score? What did the employee do to improve the score from the last performance appraisal? The comments help the employee to understand the thinking behind the score. This information is valuable for planning for the future, and is important for the employee's personnel record. It is also easier for supervisors to write appropriate, helpful comments that are tied to specific items on the forms.

Goals/Objectives

Most performance appraisals allow for articulation of work goals for the upcoming year. Employees and supervisors work together to identify goals (often referred to as "objectives.") The goals should address four areas:

- behaviors to maintain
- behaviors to improve
- activities to pursue
- knowledge to expand.

The goals can be written with specific language, designating time frames, outcomes, employee involvement, approval protocol, and so forth. Some organizations prefer that the goals be clearly detailed, holding employees accountable for completing tasks by specific deadlines. Some supervisors, however, prefer to create general goals that are referred to throughout the year, allowing employees to work with the supervisor during the year to develop tasks and achieve objectives. For example, general goals may be:

- Continue to consult weekly with Team Leaders about ISO9000 changes.
- Prepare quarterly reports submitted for review prior to deadline.

- Present three workshops at regional conferences.
- Research costs for replacement of the crane and four forklifts.

If the supervisor and the employees write the general goals together, it is essential that there be frequent meetings during the year that focus on activities, evolving timelines, and goal attainment.

Complexity

If supervisors put off completion of performance appraisals, it is usually because the forms are too long and too complicated. (Supervisors may also be avoiding the performance appraisal conversation that takes place with the employee.) A well-written performance appraisal can help to facilitate productive discussion.

Performance appraisals should be clear and concise. They should not feel to supervisors like a major term paper. The format should be easy to follow, the directions easy to understand, and the references easy to access (e.g., the descriptions of each score, the meaning of terms). It is important that supervisors be trained in the proper completion of the performance appraisal forms. If the training requires more than two hours, then the forms are too complex.

Tailoring

One of the best ways for an organization to create a tailored performance appraisal form is to gather samples from a variety of organizations and from software products. Before reviewing the collection, brainstorm about work skills that need to be evaluated, concentrating on concepts rather than exact wording. Categorize by topic (e.g., communication, leadership, teamwork, etc.) and by profession. Determine the general skills that all employees are expected to demonstrate. (Make sure that employees have been informed about the skill expectations through orientations, employee handbooks, training, and coaching sessions.)

After creating a list of skills to be measured, look through the samples of performance appraisal forms to study:

- directions
- wording

- format
- length
- organization
- time requirements
- scoring method
- signature requirements
- electronic capability.

Look for contents that match the organization's list of work skills to be evaluated. Identify approaches that can be modified to suit the organization.

Some consulting organizations and software products provide generic outlines that allow for editing and other tailoring. As a draft of the performance appraisal is created, it is essential that Human Resources/Personnel and legal representatives review the format and contents of the form.

Past And Future

The amount of emphasis placed on the past behaviors of employees depends upon the organization, but the assessment of the past should be used for discussing the future. What happened last year that can be repeated or improved upon for next year? What past experience can lead to a goal for the future? What frustrations from past events indicate the need for new training or new work strategies? Although the appraisal *form* may be used for reviewing the past year, the appraisal *meeting* should stress the plans for the upcoming work year.

There is a tendency for appraisal forms to focus solely on past work. Expectations for the future should have equal emphasis. When creating a performance appraisal form, certainly include opportunities for assessing the behaviors since the last performance appraisal. Prior goals should be reviewed for achievement. The form should then allow for new goals and objectives, plans for upcoming activities, comments about strategies for improving behavior, and ratings that justify the overall assessment and increments in pay. The understanding is that employees may have earned the appraisal results but must continue to earn them until the next appraisal.

4. WHAT SHOULD SUPERVISORS DO BEFORE THE APPRAISAL MEETING?

Preparing for the appraisal meetings takes just a few minutes, but is a crucial investment of time. Supervisors should treat the upcoming meetings seriously, taking the necessary steps to make sure that the appraisal sessions are useful, accurate, and nonthreatening. Employees should never be blindsided with brand-new information, especially negative information, that has never been discussed prior to the appraisals.

Before conducting performance appraisals, *all* employees should participate in training about the appraisal process. A cursory overview is not enough. The purpose of the training should be to emphasize that the appraisal is to build communication between the supervisors and the employees, and is an opportunity to set goals, clarify expectations, and discuss strategies for personal development. The process requires the involvement of everyone. Trainers should review the performance appraisal forms but should also present information on how to take mutual responsibility for worthwhile performance appraisal meetings.

Since supervisors have the ultimate accountability for a successful appraisal process, they should consider the following factors before the appraisal meetings:

1. Choose a private setting for the appraisal meeting, where there will be no interruptions. Seating should be comfortable, but not too informal. Supervisors should not be standing, or seated higher than the employees. The best setup is a table and chairs. If a supervisor has to sit behind a desk, it is important to place the employee's chair where papers can be read easily and the two parties can converse with good eye contact.

2. Establish an uninterrupted time frame of at least 30 minutes. Treat the employee with respect by choosing a mutually convenient time when the chances are excellent that the meeting will be able to occur. In other words, do not schedule the session right before a major project is due. Do not schedule the meeting for the last hour of the workweek, especially if it may be a stressful session. *Do not keep changing the date and time!*

Some supervisors like to take employees out to lunch and conduct the appraisal in a "relaxed" atmosphere. If going out to lunch together is routine, then it may, indeed, take the pressure off of employees and send the message that the appraisal is just a relaxed conversation. However, if the employees view the session as a rare lunch with "the boss" in a setting that is not necessarily confidential, it can create entirely too much stress for the employees. Why should employees worry about table manners and nearby customers when their work is being evaluated?

3. Plan a meeting format that can be used for all employees.

4. Review the employee's job description, or make a list of job responsibilities. Be prepared to use the performance appraisal form (completed in advance) as a source for discussing every aspect of the job. Most important, supervisors should make sure that they are very familiar with the employee's work activities. In addition to daily work, consider:

- changes in work assignments
- recent conference attendance
- organizational morale
- skill-building and training sessions
- delegated tasks
- participation in new systems, such as teamwork, computer upgrades, etc.
- changes in authority.

5. List the employee's strongest points. If necessary, ask other supervisors what positive behaviors they would include on the list.

6. Research and list any special accomplishments that have either been recognized or should be acknowledged. Keep in mind that the accomplishments do not have to be dramatic and public. A frontline worker who modifies a procedure to reduce an error rate has accomplished something significant for the organization, more than likely with little fanfare.

7. In addition to listing strong points, supervisors should create a list of skills that need attention, with notes of suggested strategies. For example, if an employee tends to get impatient when work becomes stressful, supervisors should be prepared to talk about alternative behaviors, stress management workshops, and other solutions to the problem.

One successful approach to addressing performance improvement is to consider the employee's strong points and see how they can be utilized to shore up the areas that need development. For example, if an employee is very organized but tends to get flustered when making a mistake, discuss how the organizational skills can help the employee react without stress. How can the employee create an organized series of steps to follow when a mistake occurs? Can the work area be straightened before the mistake is tackled and corrected? Can the employee analyze why the mistake occurred, in an objective, organized manner? These approaches help the employee to use organizational skills to improve other skills.

Supervisors should be prepared to point out skill areas that need work, but should have given thought to specific behaviors that can lead to improvement.

8. Too many times the work problems of employees are related to training. Poor instruction, limited training time, lack of funds, and so forth can cause employees to fail because they simply were not trained properly.

Before conducting the performance appraisal–especially before reviewing areas of improvement–be prepared to talk about the role that training has played in employee work behaviors. Since appropriate training is the responsibility of the organization, be prepared to either offer what is needed, or to find a way for the employee to be successful without training.

9. Most performance appraisal forms allow for the articulation of goals/objectives. Review the appraisal forms to determine progress and achievement of goals.

Supervisors should *not* be looking at these goals for the first time! In fact, a good appraisal meeting means that the employees and supervisor have been meeting routinely about the goals and are now ready to record that all goals have been achieved. (If not achieved, be prepared to discuss "why" and "what next.") Jot down notes about possible goals for the future. Again, at least half of the appraisal meeting should focus on the future.

10. Gather documentation to support observations made by the supervisor. Include positive recognition as well as indicators of concern. Supervisors may need:

• past appraisal forms
• memos, emails, notes
• samples of records such as safety, quality, time-on-task, error rate, etc.

- written agreements
- work samples (either role models or samples of employee work)
- assessments by colleagues (if appropriate)
- attendance records
- conference flyers, workshop descriptions, training materials that may be useful to the employee or may be evidence of attendance
- rewards, certificates, press releases, letters of invitation, customer comments, etc.

Note that these items should be quickly accessible from the employee's work file (not necessarily the formal personnel file). If the items have to be gathered from several places, start a file to save time next year!

11. Before the actual appraisal meeting, supervisors should give thought to rewards and recognition for the employee. If appropriate, tentative calculations of pay raises, possible bonuses and/or promotions, honors, etc. should be completed. It may be appropriate to discuss ideas with other managers.

Supervisors should keep an open mind. The appraisal meeting should be organized so that employees have the chance to:

- remind the supervisor of highlights of the year
- express knowledge of areas needing improvement, and plans for corrections
- provide information and documentation that could lead to a reward or recognition
- differ with the supervisor about observations, providing support for the employee's point of view.

Some organizations prefer that employees have the chance to look over their own appraisal prior to the appraisal meeting. Other organizations ask employees to complete a blank form to prepare answers to questions such as:

- How do you contribute to organizational goals?
- What are your strongest skills?
- What steps will you take to improve skills:
- What would you like to accomplish next year?

If the session is a true dialogue, then the supervisor may learn new information and may change initial thoughts on assessment ratings and rewards and recognition. Supervisors should be prepared for the possibility of making a case, listening, weighing information, waiting to decide, confirming a decision, or actually changing the original position.

12. It helps supervisors if they know the ultimate goals of the appraisal session ahead of time. What essential points must be conveyed? What messages *must* get across?

Supervisors should know, in advance, what the objectives of the meetings are and plan on routinely coming back to those objectives. Does the supervisor want to make sure that an employee finally understands the seriousness of some of the work behaviors? Does the supervisor want the employee to feel encouraged and willing to try new things? Does the supervisor want an employee to change one bad work habit so that all other areas will improve?

13. Complete the performance appraisal, allowing time to look it over again before the meeting. Make personal notes about appraisal questions that need further discussion. Consider the questions that may cause concern or that may require documentation. Highlight the questions that show strong skills and positive behaviors. Consult with other supervisors if necessary. Be prepared for presenting an overall picture of the appraisal. After preparing for the performance appraisal, the supervisor should ask two more questions:

- What have I done to contribute to the work behaviors of the employee? (This could be positive or negative.)
- What can I offer to do in the future to help the employee to improve behaviors and achieve goals?

Excellent supervisors can comfortably look in the mirror and openly assess their own role in guiding and supporting employees.

5. WHAT ARE THE QUALITIES OF AN EXCELLENT PERFORMANCE APPRAISAL MEETNG?

The purpose of an appraisal meeting is for the employees and supervisor to review the past and plan the future. An excellent meeting includes a supervisor who is well prepared and well versed in the work of the employee, and willing to discuss openly, listening to employee concerns and ideas. The meeting also has an employee who is well prepared to provide information and documentation, and is willing to discuss openly with the supervisor and listen to suggestions.

Components of Successful Appraisal Meetings

- appraisal conducted on time, when the appraisal is due
- a comfortable, relaxed atmosphere that is focused and helpful
- thorough preparation
- supervisor self-evaluation
- a clearly articulated purpose
- information based on facts, not on gossip or assumptions
- an unbiased, fair approach, not based on comparisons with others
- documentation of observations
- strengths praised and rewarded
- areas of improvement turned into objectives
- targets, goals, plans established for the future
- mutual agreements established, with written results.

Supervisors who understand that employees are better able to listen to the appraisal results if they are comfortable, make every effort to:

- physically face the employee and maintain eye contact
- set and maintain a tone of support and problem-solving
- stop often to listen and restate questions and concerns to show understanding
- read body language to determine the employee's emotions and to put the employee at ease
- wait to conclude, making sure that the employee's perspectives have been heard and discussed.

---

6. WHAT ARE THE STEPS TO CONDUCTING AN APPRAISAL MEETING?

The process of the performance appraisal meeting depends primarily upon the relationship between the supervisor and the employees.

The meetings may be quick and to the point, or may involve lengthy conversations. There may be tension, or everyone may be completely at ease. But, regardless of the relationship, it is important for supervisors to try to conduct all performance appraisal meetings in the same fashion. The time allotted, the preparation, and the format should be about the same for all employees.

The following are general guidelines for supervisors for conducting the meeting:

1. Explain the purpose of the meeting and the format that will be followed. Make sure that there is mutual agreement that the outcome of the meeting should be to arrive at an assessment of the past, and plans for the future. Give the employees a sense of how much time has been scheduled for the session, but do not pressure them to conclude the meeting by a specified time. It is certainly acceptable to alert the employees that another appointment or meeting is scheduled, but leave plenty of time to talk in case the appraisal meeting hits some snags.

2. Get right to the point. If the overall appraisal is positive, then say so. *Then* mention that areas needing improvement will be addressed in the meeting. Highlight the positive examples right away, then quickly summarize the areas that need improvement. This approach puts the employees at ease because the general appraisal results are right out on the table. Explain that the details will be discussed while going over the appraisal form.

If the overall appraisal is negative (or there are strong areas needing improvement), mention strengths immediately and quickly. Then stress confidence that the employees will work on areas needing improvement. Describe these areas quickly. Do not spend a lot of time praising, only to suddenly hit employees with bad news. Give the employees time to digest that there are weak spots that will be discussed. Say what they are right away. Reassure the employees that everyone has skills that need attention, and that you will work with the employees to define those areas that need improvement and create objectives. Repeat the strengths and begin going over the entire appraisal.

Keep in mind that employees will probably walk out of the appraisal meeting remembering the very positive statements and the very negative statements. The rest of the session may not be as memorable. Make sure that the positives are repeated often and that the negatives are framed in a context of creating objectives and plans for the future. Employees should leave knowing exactly what they need to do next.

3. Ask the employees if there is a specific issue that they feel should be discussed right away. The employees will not be able to concentrate if a question or concern is not resolved at the beginning of the session.

4. Walk through the written appraisal. If you have already summarized the appraisal verbally, then reviewing the written forms step-by-step provides documentation and explanations, and employees are not sitting in the meeting wondering what is around the corner.

5. Keep in mind the main message that you want to get across to the employee. Perhaps you want the employee to take more initiative, concentrate on improving a skill area, or assume additional responsibility. Introduce the key point and keep reinforcing it.

6. With proper preparation, each item on the appraisal should be supported with either an explanation or written documentation. If the employee agrees with the assessment, add some praise and move on. If the employee seems to be hesitant in agreeing, then start listening. Wait until the employee reacts and do not immediately reinforce your point. Be ready to consider another perspective.

Then explain:

Here is what I was thinking. . .
That sheds a different light. . .
Here is what I have observed. . .
I am still concerned. . .
I had not considered that factor. . .

No matter whether you agree with the employee or not, conclude with:

Why don't we pin this down by creating a goal for next year?

If the employee and supervisor are concentrating on writing a goal that makes sense to both of them, then the supervisor is successful in making a point, and the employee has some control over the level of improvement. This approach moves away from debate and concentrates on resolving the issue by creating a plan.

7. Keep creating goals. Even if the final document only contains one or two written goals (or if the form does not allow for goal-writing), create them together for future reference.

8. Remember that if the supervisor has been observing work behaviors all year long, has consulted with colleagues, and has thoroughly prepared for the appraisal session, then the appraisal documents should be on target. There really should be few changes. But the meeting is a chance for employees to remind supervisors about accomplishments, provide information that the supervisor may not know, and explain the rationale for work behaviors. Supervisors should be prepared to discuss, *listen*, and perhaps alter the results to reflect the perspective of the employees.

Most supervisors cannot observe employees all of the time. They may misunderstand behaviors they see at work, or may not know the background of an event. Employees should have the chance to explain. As each skill area is reviewed, consider the overall picture, listen to the employees (even if the tone is defensive), and be prepared to occasionally compromise or make a change in the appraisal. If it is truly a joint effort, the employees will be much more committed to improving behaviors and working toward goals.

9. Conclude with formalities (signing the document, calculating overall scores, and so forth) always followed by informal praise and encouragement.

---

7. WHAT DO EMPLOYEES WANT FROM A PERFORMANCE APPRAISAL MEETING?

When employees are asked about an upcoming appraisal meeting with their supervisor, they tend to say, *"I hope that my supervisor does not:*

> . . . reschedule again."
> . . . allow interruptions and take phone calls."
> . . . act bored or in a hurry."
> . . . do all of the talking."
> . . . avoid talking about my concerns."
> . . . stress problems, forgetting about the good work that I have done."
> . . . surprise me with something that I never knew about."

Above all, employees would like the appraisals to be fair, and conducted on time. There may be ambivalence about discussing the appraisal results, but waiting and wondering can be even more stressful. Supervisors should meet appraisal deadlines even if they do not necessarily look forward to the meetings. (Some companies have been known to deduct supervisor pay for every late day.) Since one of the purposes of the performance appraisal process is to build communication between the supervisors and employees, it is up to the supervisors to complete the forms and initiate the scheduling of the meeting.

Supervisors may also find the performance appraisal process stressful, especially if they have to deliver news that may not be what employees expected. Supervisors can get frustrated when they thoroughly prepare for the appraisal and have taken the process seriously, only to hear the employees express unreasonable expectations. Some employees see the appraisal meeting as an opportunity to unload complaints and make demands. Some employees do not say a great deal during the session, only to complain later to coworkers. To ease tension and promote productive dialogue, supervisors should establish the purpose of the meeting at the very beginning, and set a tone that encourages focused discussion. If employees need the time to vent frustrations or criticize different aspects of the organization (including people), supervisors should keep turning concerns into goals, with supervisory strategies that can assist the employee in meeting those goals. Employees will be more willing to establish goals if they feel that the process was fair.

At the conclusion of the appraisal meeting, supervisors should feel confident that employees know:

- how they are doing
- what they can do to improve
- how the supervisor will help
- how will ongoing feedback occur
- what are plans for the future
- how goal achievement will be monitored
- what happens to the written appraisal
- what recognition or rewards will occur.

8. SHOULD PERFORMANCE APPRAISALS BE TIED TO MONEY?

If a performance appraisal process is designed to provide employees a fair assessment of their work in the past, as well as realistic plans for the future, then attaching money to the appraisal may complicate the process. The emphasis inevitably becomes the bonus, the increment, the raise, the monetary reward. Employees see the purpose of the appraisal meeting solely as the opportunity to find out about future paychecks. Supervisors spend most of their preparation time on justifying financial decisions.

In organizations where supervisors have discretion in determining pay raises, the appraisal process can become centered around maneuvering the appraisal results to fit the raise or bonus. For example, if a supervisor believes that one employee, Jack, has had another outstanding year and deserves financial recognition, there may be a tendency to score areas of improvement a little higher. Then Jack will be guaranteed to receive his raise, but he will not necessarily be aware of behaviors that could use improvement.

Or suppose Mary Ann has also had a terrific year, but just cannot compete with Jack's experience and positive reputation. Should Mary Ann receive a pay raise equivalent to Jack's because of her hard work and growth, or should she expect to receive less than Jack because she is newer on the job and not as well known? These questions can result in ethical dilemmas for the supervisors, often resulting in performance appraisals that are based on comparisons and the "bottom line" rather than on actual work performance. The key is to create a performance appraisal system that is fair and unbiased, allowing monetary decisions to emerge because the format provides clear results. Suggested approaches are:

• If a performance appraisal includes a rating system that results in a final total score, then the pay increments tied to the total score can be decided in advance. For example, if an employee receives a "60" as a total score, it is predetermined that the raise is 4 percent, if a "70," then the raise is 4.5 percent, and so forth.

Of course, supervisors may still manipulate the scores if they truly want an employee to receive a certain amount of money. But if the figures are calculated before the completion of the appraisal, and the criteria for rating employees is specific, there is a much better chance of creating a clear and fair monetary determination.

• Some supervisors are given a specific amount of money and are to determine how to divide it up among employees. This process can be more challenging than preestablished formulas. Again, if all of the appraisals are completed and then ranked by results, it is less complicated to determine pay increases. Supervisors are advised to create a tentative distribution that can be discussed with other supervisors who are familiar with the work of the employees. Once the employees are ranked, the question centers around the percentage per person. Some supervisors decide ahead of time the amount each level of the ranking will receive, no matter who the employee may be. The top employee will receive a 5 percent increment, the second highest will receive 4.5 percent, and so forth. This protects the supervisor from being influenced by personal preferences once the money has to be distributed.

• Some organizations stress "pay for performance" with increments tied directly to goal achievement, behavioral development, and/or exceptional accomplishments. Appraisals from the past year include written expectations that are worth either a specific number of points or an increment percentage. Employees spend the year carrying out activities to meet the expectations. Evidence of success is either described in the appraisal or evaluated when the activities have been completed. Accomplishments are totaled and pay increases determined.

This process can provide an incentive for employees to perform well, but the distribution of awards (the payments) can be arbitrary and subjective. If employees did not achieve a goal because of organizational problems, then how is pay determined? Should it be "no pay if no performance?" Or what if employees go beyond the expected results, neglecting other work? The performance in one area was exceptional, so how is pay determined?

To be successful at true "pay for performance," the goals must be specific and revisited throughout the year. They should include the outcome, activities, timeline, and measure of accomplishment. Modifications may be necessary so that employees can be rewarded for accomplishments that may not have met the initial expectations, but are still noteworthy. The entire process should also allow for employee creativity and initiative, as well as for steady, step-by-step achievement.

• Some organizations connect appraisals and money, but allow time to elapse after the appraisal, before administering pay increases. This allows employees and supervisors to discuss and revise the appraisals and to set goals together, without focusing on the financial results. Emphasis is on performance development and objectives for the coming year.

After two to three months, the pay increases are determined. Supervisors have a chance to conduct all annual appraisals, review the overall results, observe employee follow-up behavior, and take the necessary time to contemplate monetary decisions. This process seems to work well because it gives supervisors distance from the process so they are able to seriously reflect upon the impact their decisions will have on employee paychecks, and can feel confident that the decisions were well justified.

Employees, of course, realize that the performance appraisal will ultimately affect their pay increase, but at least for the appraisal meeting they can concentrate on reviewing the past and planning for the future.

It is imperative that if supervisors are going to tie money to appraisals that they not be influenced by the personal situations of the employees. It may be tempting to provide higher increases to those who appear to need it the most, but raises should be based on work performance and appraisal results only.

9. WHAT ARE BARRIERS TO A SUCCESSFUL APPRAISAL?

Supervisors should try to avoid the following barriers to a successful performance appraisal meeting:

Recent-Behavior Syndrome

Performance appraisals are supposed to be a summary of accomplishments from past months, and a list of goals for the future, not a reaction to something (good or bad) that occurred recently. Coaching should have already been conducted to address recent behaviors. Current events can certainly be included in the overall appraisal, but should not be the focal point.

Longevity Bias

Length of employment should not influence appraisal contents if standards are clear and forms are well written. Whether employees are new or have been working for the organization for a long time, they should be evaluated in comparison to the standards, not in comparison to other employees. Assumptions should not be made based on the age of the employee or length of employment. Expectations should be consistent across the board, regardless of the amount of time in the job or at the organization.

Halos And Horns

"Halos and horns" is a phrase that is often used to describe supervisory response to *one incident.*

The "halo" effect refers to a situation when an employee did something very positive and noticeable once, and has earned credit for it ever since. The "halo" appraisal is based on the assumption that the employee will continue to repeat the excellent work, even if there is evidence otherwise. In fact, some supervisors who are influenced by the "halo" effect believe that exceptional behavior in one area can imply exceptional behavior in all areas. For example, a supervisor may assume that an employee who made a strong presentation has good general communication skills in all aspects of work. The performance appraisal may reflect the assumption rather than the reality.

If an employee makes a major mistake (even if it was years ago), the negative image (or "horns") can remain. For example, an employee may freeze during an important presentation, or make a mistake on the production line. Even when the incident is long over and corrections have been made, supervisors can be influenced by the "horn" effect by including reference to the incident, or by evaluating the employee with the assumption that the mistake will be repeated.

When conducting appraisals, supervisors should consider whether they are being influenced by "halos" and "horns."

Supervisor Resistance

Some supervisors may resist the appraisal process because they are concerned that the evaluations are actually an assessment of the supervisor. If an employee does poorly on the appraisal, does it mean that the supervisor has failed? In organizations that have a climate of tension, this concern may be legitimate. Supervisors should make sure that regular meetings with struggling employees have been documented, and that conferences about the employees have been held with other managers long before the date of the performance appraisal.

The distribution of appraisal results should show that employees vary in their skills and goal achievement, even if all the employees are excellent workers and are achieving goals. Appraisal comments should make it clear that supervisors will continue to play a key role in improving employee performance. If supervisors insist on creating appraisals so that they personally look good, they need to review the purpose of the performance appraisal process.

Supervisors may also resist "judging" employees, especially if their word will determine the financial status or future role of the employees. If supervisors understand the purpose of the appraisal process as an opportunity to assist employees, then the process does not seem quite as judgmental. Ongoing conversations about work skills and goals make the formal performance appraisal an expected summary, rather than a final judgment.

Everyone Is Satisfactory

Occasionally supervisors avoid the challenge of conducting performance appraisals by giving everyone approximately the same assessment. Even though this approach may make the supervisors feel comfortable, it can often backfire. Employees who have worked hard and feel that they have earned an excellent appraisal will resent an average assessment, especially if low-achieving employees receive the same results. Employees who need to improve performance may not get the message.

Supervisors may find some aspects of the appraisal process nerve-wracking, but if they follow the steps to a fair and productive appraisal, they can be honest in the appraisal and the process can be useful and comfortable for everyone involved.

10. WHAT IF PROBLEMS ARISE DURING THE PERFORMANCE APPRAISAL MEETING?

Not every appraisal meeting will run smoothly. Sometimes problems arise that can make supervisors feel as if they have lost control of the meeting. Some typical problems are:

Disagreement About Results

Know in advance if employees must sign their appraisals as an indication of agreement with the contents. Supervisors should be able to support appraisal scores and comments with evidence. If an employee does not agree (or simply will not accept the evidence), determine whether a compromise is in the best interest of the employee. Since one of the purposes of appraisals is to clarify standards and expectations, it might be better to stick to the initial appraisal. Comments written by both the supervisor and the employee can be attached to the appraisal, or Human Resources/Personnel can conduct a separate meeting for the purpose of establishing new behavioral goals. Emphasis throughout the appraisal meeting should be on the areas that were agreed upon by both parties, with renewed emphasis at the conclusion of the session. Building relationships is a critical aspect of the appraisal process.

Someone Is Not Listening

Supervisors should be doing less than 25 percent of the talking in a performance appraisal meeting. As the employees are talking, the supervisors should be listening attentively, taking notes if necessary, and showing interest by asking follow-up questions. Remember, this is an opportunity for the employees to get individual attention. Stop talking and *listen.*

It may be the employees who are not listening. Perhaps they feel compelled to explain activities, defend behaviors, or inform the supervisor about accomplishments. They may not be willing to listen because the appraisal is less than satisfactory.

Supervisors have more success in gaining the full attention of the employees if they are:

- Reiterating information that had been provided during coaching and other prior interactions
- Specific about *what is expected*, not dwelling on what is wrong or how evidence was gathered
- Willing to ask the employees open-ended questions such as:
  What do you think?
  Does that make sense to you?
  What would you like to do to improve this?
- Prepared with a tentative goal that can be discussed and finely tuned.

Sometimes it is necessary to let the employees "vent" for a few minutes. Venting emotions can be helpful for both parties as sensitive issues are brought out into the open, but supervisors should always concentrate on establishing a goal that addresses the problem and gives the employees direction. If the employees are still not capable of listening and accepting the appraisal, the supervisor has to decide whether to renegotiate the appraisal results or stand firm. The decision should be based on what is best for establishing the employee as a value to the organization.

The Employee Is Not Talking

If it is possible that employees will be quiet and uncomfortable in the meeting (regardless of all efforts to put the employees at ease), it is a good idea to ask the employees to prepare notes ahead of time. Ask the employees to complete the appraisal form, jot down answers to a few questions or make lists of accomplishments and goals.

If employees are surprisingly quiet, then they may:

- be listening and thinking
- be waiting for the other "shoe to drop"
- have something unrelated on their minds
- be emotional
- be bored!

It is not necessary to fill the silence with talking. Make sure that it is clear that comments and questions are welcome throughout the session, and that employees will be given time to absorb the information Pause often. Then the employees can begin to relax, and share what is on their minds. If necessary, agree to meet again, after the employees have had a chance to prepare responses.

Evidence Is Not Clear

Some work, especially at the management level, is hard to measure. It is less tangible and the activities "behind the scenes" may not be as obvious as the outcomes.

Since performance appraisals are based on behaviors, competencies, and goals, the supervisors and employees should define together what should be evaluated. They should then determine the evidence that will demonstrate success. What will be considered proof of employee involvement in a project? What will be an indicator of skills such as planning, mediation, or teamwork? Will a final product be evidence of leadership, quality standards, and problem-solving abilities?

Sometimes the end result may appear to be the only means of determining if the employees have done their jobs. The steps in between cannot actually be measured, even if it is the bulk of the work. Ask the employees what would be indications that the appropriate steps are being taken. Keep in mind that incomplete projects, missed deadlines, or poor results may not be related to the work behaviors of the employees but rather to organizational problems. For skills that are hard to measure, it is essential to establish expectations early on and to look at the entire organizational picture before completing appraisals.

Everyone Is Excellent

Congratulations! There is no rule that says that supervisors must have a distribution of scores on performance appraisals. If all employees are excellent, then give them credit. (First make sure that the performance appraisal is actually measuring performance.) Then the supervisors should give themselves a little credit for successful hiring, coaching, training, and managing.

Employees Get Emotional

Employees may get emotional as they review their appraisals. The emotional reaction may be planned or unintentional. Employees may cry, get angry, arrive with piles of "evidence," argue, or express disdain or sarcasm. It is essential that supervisors explain the purpose of the meeting and review the highlights of the appraisal immediately. Give employees the opportunity to express what is on their minds. Otherwise, the content of the meeting will not be retained. Sometimes emotional outbursts can be quite revealing. If supervisors listen seriously, refrain from getting defensive, and try to turn the concerns into a goal that makes sense to both parties, the meeting can get refocused.

If an employee cannot seem to regain self-control, then take a short break, make it clear that the behavior needs to be brought under control, and plan on meeting *very soon*. Give the employee a quiet space to calm down, and discourage interaction with other employees since it may inspire others to create a scene. Do not wait too long to meet again because the employee may continue to build up emotion and rally support from coworkers, or may be embarrassed and anxious to apologize.

It is important to remember that stress can build up before appraisal meetings. Keep a box of tissues handy and articulate a plan to end the meeting with agreed-upon goals.

Advancement Is Limited

On occasion, excellent employees cannot be rewarded with promotions, or employees who are working hard to improve and grow may not see future advancement opportunities. Supervisors should be prepared to provide rewards and recognition in other ways. There are hundreds of ways to acknowledge the accomplishments of employees and to encourage them to stay with the organization, many at no cost to the organization. Conduct research into alternatives to advancement such as delegation of new projects, cross-training, conference presentations, awards, perks, bonuses and prizes, challenging projects, leadership assignments, and so forth (see Chapter 7).

Both Parties Are Friends

If a supervisor has to evaluate coworkers who are also friends, it is important to talk to the coworkers about possible conflicts *before* the forms are completed. Discuss how the appraisal will be done on the basis of standards that are established and evidence that has been accumulated. Acknowledge openly that the process may feel awkward at first, but the process will be conducted in the same way for all employees.

It is not a good idea to blindside employees with unforeseen negative appraisals, regardless of whether the employees are friends or not. Continuous feedback and coaching can establish relationships that can be professional and friendly at the same time. The performance appraisal should just be another step in the process of providing feedback.

Supervisors may also have to indicate that the appraisal discussion must be limited to the meeting time, even though it may be tempting to discuss the appraisal when socializing. Limits to discussions will be determined by the relationship and the culture of the organization.

Confidentiality Is A Concern

Confidentiality cannot be guaranteed when conducting performance appraisals. It is inevitable that employees will share results with coworkers, friends, or family. Supervisors may have to discuss results with management. Ask employees to refrain from discussing their appraisal (especially if it is tied to money), but do not expect 100 percent compliance with the request.

---

11. WHAT HAPPENS TO WRITTEN PERFORMANCE APPRAISALS?

Most organizations keep the final written appraisal results in the personnel files of the employees. The appraisals are considered to be formal documents that can be used by Human Resources/Personnel and management for decisions about employee retention, promotion, and termination.

Organizations have to establish their own guidelines about the accessibility of appraisals, as well as whether they are considered legal documents owned by the organization. Some questions to consider are:

- Should the documents be signed? By whom?
- What if an employee refuses to sign the document?
- Where will the appraisals be stored?
- Will copies be distributed to the employees and the evaluating supervisors?
- Who will have access to the appraisals?
- Can the appraisal be used as a reference tool?
- Can the appraisals be used in employment/union hearings?
- Will appraisals be destroyed if employees resign or are terminated from employment?

It is important that these questions be resolved *before* implementation of a performance appraisal system.

Chapter 5

THE TRUTH ABOUT 360° ASSESSMENTS

I had no idea.
(Accounting Supervisor, responding to the results of a 360° Assessment.)

Most supervisors are evaluated by their bosses. The performance appraisal forms are filled out by the boss only, and it is the boss who determines if the supervisor's work has been satisfactory, if there are work behaviors that need improving, and if a raise or bonus is warranted.

Traditional performance appraisal meetings (or "reviews," "evaluations," or "assessments") are usually limited to the boss and the supervisor. But the observations of the boss are only one perspective.

There is another approach to evaluating supervisors, the 360° assessment. In this approach, the organization recognizes that many workers are aware of the supervisor's performance, and they should all have the opportunity to provide feedback.

In a 360° assessment (referred to as a "360"), the boss evaluates, and so do coworkers. A supervisor who is the subject of a 360 will be evaluated by other supervisors (or "peers"), by all of the bosses who are familiar with the work of the supervisor, and by employees who are being supervised. In some 360 assessments, the supervisor even completes a *self*-evaluation to compare with the perspectives of coworkers.

Since the 360 is for performance development it is also used to evaluate Team Leaders, Senior Managers, and other employees. It is *not* intended to be a formal appraisal, but a tool for identifying specific areas of improvement in work behaviors. It provides thorough feedback, so that those who are evaluated are aware of how their work habits and behaviors affect everyone around them. It is a valuable resource for determining exactly what behaviors need modification, and what skills are respected and appreciated.

The 360 must be conducted carefully, because coworkers evaluating each other can be a sensitive process. This chapter provides realistic, detailed information on the design and implementation of a 360° assessment program.

1. WHAT EXACTLY IS A 360?

A "360" is an assessment system that is used to evaluate employees. It is usually used to evaluate managers, but can also be used for evaluating Team Leaders, senior executives, supervisors, frontline employees, or other staff. The results are used for employee development and goal-setting.

The 360 is different than other evaluation systems because it involves gathering written feedback from just about anyone who interacts on a regular basis with the employee being evaluated. Copies of the same form are given to all evaluators, known as "raters."

For example, suppose Judy is a manager of a shipping department, and it is time for her performance appraisal. If the organization uses a 360, then Judy will be evaluated by her boss, her coworkers at the same level ("peers"), and the people that she supervises. She may also be evaluated by her customers, as well as vendors, truck drivers, and dispatchers, if they are particularily familiar with Judy's work. All of these raters could complete an evaluation form. All of the evaluation forms are combined into one report.

Some 360 systems give the employees the opportunity to assess themselves. They can then compare their personal perspective with the perspectives of coworkers.

Think of a circle (measuring 360 degrees), and put the employee who is being evaluated right in the center. Everyone around the employee would be considered a good source of feedback and may be asked to complete a 360 assessment form.

2. HOW CAN THE RESULTS BE USED?

The 360 assessment is supposed to be used as a developmental tool, giving employees a chance to focus on areas that need improvement.

Although it may be used as a formal evaluation system, the real purpose of the 360 is to gather feedback from multiple sources and identify how employees can do a better job. It is also used to recognize and reward employees for positive work performance.

It is most effective when the subject of the 360 (the person being evaluated) can discuss the results with a supervisor and make a performance action plan for the future.

3. WHAT TERMS ARE USED IN THE 360 PROCESS?

In the lexicon of 360 assessments:
Subject: the person being evaluated
Rater: the person doing the evaluating
(sometimes all of the raters are referred to as the "stakeholders")
Peer: a rater who is at the same level in the organization as the subject (such as a supervisor evaluating another supervisor)
Boss: any rater who supervises the subject (such as a vice president evaluating a manager)
Team/Employees/Staff/Direct Reports: those raters who are evaluating their supervisors or a subject located above them in the organizational hierarchy (such as a senior manager)
External Rater: a customer, client, vendor, etc. who does business with the subject's organization on a regular basis

Note that sometimes 360 assessments are referred to as "multi-rater feedback," "full-circle," "peer review," or "upward appraisals." These are not particularly accurate terms, but they do show up in the literature.

4. HOW IS THE 360 USUALLY IMPLEMENTED?

Many organizations, especially smaller companies, create their own 360 system, including devising the evaluation forms that will be used.

There are also companies that offer guidance and software systems for implementing a 360 assessment program. If purchasing such a system, it is important to choose a system that will meet the goals of the organization and will provide information that is useful to the subject. Once there is a better understanding of the process, it is easier to determine the best resource to use.

Usually an organization will follow the steps below. ***Tips for implementing the steps are described in further detail in the sections that follow.***

1. Determine if the organizational philosophy and culture can support the 360 concept.
2. Identify the people who are going to be evaluated (the "subjects").
3. Determine who will evaluate them (the "raters").
4. Identify or create the evaluation forms that will be used.
5. Determine a time frame for completion of the forms.
6. Determine a process for disseminating and collecting the forms.
7. Determine what will be done with the results.
8. Check the entire process for fairness and confidentiality.
9. Set up a pilot.
10. Explain the entire process to the subjects and raters.
11. Test run the 360 and make adjustments.
12. Conduct the 360 for a larger group.
13. Share results individually with subjects.
14. Follow up with plans for performance improvement.
15. Follow up with recognition for positive results.

5. DO 360s WORK?

A 360 feedback system can be very helpful to employees if it is carried out carefully.

Too often traditional performance appraisals consist of the boss meeting privately with the employee, giving just the supervisor's perspective on work performance. The point of the 360 is to get many different perspectives.

If 360s are done well, subjects can find out exactly what they need to work on in the future. They can receive specific information about their work skills and behaviors, and learn how they are viewed by different groups. The boss, or supervisor, may have one point of view, but peers may see work performance differently.

For example, a Team Leader may discover from the 360 results that the boss always feels well informed, and considers the Team Leader's communication to be excellent. The team, however, may provide feedback that they feel left out of the loop because the Team Leader focuses on communicating with the boss! Now the Team Leader knows that communication with the team has to improve.

Subjects can also find out where they excel. Many employees have been pleased to discover from 360 results that coworkers recognize improvement and specific skills. Their strengths may be acknowledged, resulting in positive reinforcement directly from colleagues.

6. CAN 360s BACKFIRE?

Yes. 360 assessment systems can backfire if they do not have:

- a fair process for identifying evaluators (or "raters") who truly know the work behaviors of the person being evaluated
- clear instructions to raters
- quick, easy forms to complete
- attention to confidentiality
- a time frame that allows for quick and efficient gathering of evaluations
- clear definition of staff involvement in the 360 process
- a plan for following up on the results
- policies for protecting the records, handling grievances related to the results, and allowing access to the data (as with any other performance review system).

In addition, subjects may be uncomfortable being evaluated by people who are unaware of their accomplishments, who may not like them personally, or who do not have much say about raises and promotions.

Raters may feel uncomfortable filling out forms about their colleagues, especially if they have some negative things to say. On the other hand, they may take advantage of the opportunity to unload their negative opinions. This can be especially damaging if the subject did not see it coming.

The entire 360 process should be explained in detail, giving employees enough time to digest the information and ask questions. (In other words, do not suddenly send out an evaluation form without warning.) The protection of the privacy of employees and the use of the data should be clear.

The key is to recognize that the feedback is a composite picture and is a resource for determining what to do next. If the employee has a pattern of weak spots that are revealed by the 360 assessment, then the next step is to figure out a plan for eliminating those weak spots. Ideally, this plan is created by the employee working with a supervisor who can help with strategies and techniques.

7. CAN 360s BE BIASED?

Although it is not possible to eliminate all bias in the process, there are ways of ensuring that the results of the 360s will be fair. Keep in mind that raters may:

- hesitate before being completely forthright about a coworker's weaknesses
- worry about being discovered as the rater who gave negative responses
- not want to get involved in evaluating a subject who is known to be struggling (especially if they feel that the 360 will provide documentation for discipline or termination)
- see the 360 as a chance to shed a bad light on a subject who is competition
- see the 360 as a chance to exaggerate a subject's strengths because of a personal relationship.

These are just some of the ways that the process can quickly become biased.

However, standard appraisal procedures can also be riddled with bias. Not all supervisors approach the traditional performance appraisal process with an open, unbiased mind. A 360 can at least gather from a variety of sources so that bias can be reduced.

If it appears that the organization has a culture that promotes fierce internal competition, blame, second-guessing, and other behaviors that pit employees against one another, then it may not be advisable to attempt a 360 assessment approach. In fact, it might be necessary to work on creating a more comfortable culture before attempting any type of appraisal process.

Bias can be reduced by:

- using a process to select raters that will provide a thorough, fair picture of performance.
- paying close attention to confidentiality.
- presenting information to raters about how they may be unintentionally biased, and how they should concentrate on the behaviors they have personally witnessed, preferably over the last year. They are not rating the subject on personal life, on relationships and past history, or on what they have heard. They should skip any parts that they cannot answer with confidence.

On occasion, raters may indicate that they do not feel qualified to complete the assessment form, or they feel that their relationship with the subject will bias the results (negatively or positively). They may be excluded if that seems appropriate, but their primary task is to give their own personal perspective on the work behaviors that they have observed. These observations will be combined with several others so that a broad picture of behavior can be obtained.

Peers may hesitate to be honest about coworkers at the same level. Subjects completing a *self-evaluation* form may be concerned about evaluating themselves too high or too low, especially if their supervisor may misconstrue the results. All of these concerns can be appeased if the process is explained thoroughly, and if supervisors are well trained on how to interpret and discuss results. Emphasis should always be on the goal of creating a composite picture of work behaviors.

Of course, not everyone will be completely comfortable. But the overall results can be informative and any "outliers" or scores that seem to stand out can be discussed with the supervisor.

8. WHEN IS AN ORGANIZATION PREPARED TO IMPLEMENT A 360?

The design and implementation of a 360 assessment can be a nightmare if the organization has not created a plan and analyzed several different aspects of the program. Why a nightmare? For starters, a 360 can be logistically complex; a poorly crafted assessment can be useless to the employees or the leadership; and the 360 results can be misinterpreted or misused. But with careful planning it can be a valuable tool for both the subjects and the organization. This chapter addresses the difficulties of implementing a 360, and provides information that can help organizations to plan a 360 assessment process. In order to avoid potential hazards, it is recommended that the organization make decisions about the following questions before getting started:

What is our purpose for the 360?
What will be done with the results?

It is essential that these two questions be settled first. Once the organization is comfortable with the purpose and the application of the 360 assessment, the following questions should be addressed:

- *Who needs to be briefed on the purpose and process of the 360?*
- *Who will be evaluated?*
- *Will it be voluntary or mandatory?*
- *Will there be a pilot group?*
- *How many coworkers will complete the assessments, and from what levels of the organization?*
- *Who will be the primary contact person to oversee the process?*
- *Will outside sources be utilized?*
- *How will senior management demonstrate support for the 360 process?*
- *What assessment forms will be used?*
- *Will employees/unions be involved in designing the assessments?*
- *Will quantitative assessments be supplemented by narrative, other performance reviews, or interviews?*
- *What resources (time, money, support staff, technology) will be needed?*
- *How will confidentiality be maintained?*
- *What if a rater hesitates to complete the form?*

- *How will the assessments be administered, gathered, and summarized?*
- *What will the subjects receive?*
- *Will entire groups be summarized?*
- *Who will see the results?*
- *What will be done with results that need special attention?*
- *Who will get a copy of the results?*
- *How will the results be discussed with the subjects?*
- *Who will need training in action plan development?*
- *What resources are needed for following up on results?*
- *What will be the time frame for the entire process?*
- *How will the entire 360 process be evaluated to see if it was successful?*

An organization is not prepared to implement a 360 if employee confidence has not been taken into consideration. If the employees are concerned that the results will be used deliberately for criticism and discipline, that the process will lack confidentiality, or that the assessment form or selection of raters will be biased, then the organization is not ready.

Of course, some employees will be skeptical, especially if the direction to participate in a 360 comes from senior levels, with little explanation. It is essential that the purpose and process of the 360 be explained, allowing employees to share questions and concerns. An organization is ready if it can genuinely inform employees that they are utilizing 360s for the purpose of employee development, as well as employee recognition. Sharing specific information about how the results will be stored and reviewed is critical.

A vital determinant of success of 360 assessments is the attitude of senior leaders. Enthusiasm and support for the process, clear communication, and thorough follow-through are essential.

9. WHO SHOULD BE EVALUATED?

A 360 can be part of an ongoing performance review process, used whenever an employee is scheduled for an appraisal. It can also be a mass evaluation so that patterns of strengths and weaknesses across a large group can be determined. For example, one organization conducted 360 assessments on all supervisors for the sole purpose of defining future training needs.

Before determining the subjects, decide how the results will be used. If it is a developmental tool, then new supervisors may be the initial target group, or experienced managers may benefit from feedback from a variety of coworkers, rather than from one boss.

A 360 should not be used for promoting an employee from a group of competing subjects. For example, if there is a lucrative opening in the Marketing Department and only in-house candidates are undergoing a 360 review, it may look like the results will be used to determine who gets the new job. Raters figure out very quickly that they may have someone's future in their hands, and they could either be uncomfortable with that power—or really relish it! It is best to stay away from using a 360 to determine who gets the next promotion.

However, the results can certainly be added to the collection of information on an employee, but *only if behavior after discussion of the results* is also taken into consideration. For example, perhaps the assessment results showed that a supervisor could benefit from a conflict resolution class to gain assistance in supervising a difficult team of employees. Did the supervisor take the class and use the information to mediate team problems? The *follow-up* to the 360 should be emphasized.

If this is the first attempt at 360 assessments, it is best to start with a small group. No matter what the size of the group, a database will have to be established in order to keep track of the assessments and the results. Once the number of subjects reaches 25, it is best to have a support system that can process the data, such as a software package specifically designed for 360 assessments.

10. HOW DO YOU DETERMINE WHO WILL DO THE EVALUATING?

This is tricky. The goal is to select coworkers at different levels of the organization who will give a fair assessment based on their knowledge of the subject and their desire to promote employee development. It is advisable to keep the list of raters under 20 people or the process can become cumbersome, especially for those who are evaluating several coworkers.

It is important that subjects are evaluated by raters who are familiar with their work, even if it is just one aspect of their work. For example, suppose Sam handles purchase orders and interacts with anyone who submits a purchase order. But his colleagues in the Accounting Department, the engineers who work with Sam on ordering equipment for capital projects, and the shipping supervisor are also familiar with how well Sam performs crucial parts of his job. Sam's list should include those individuals, especially since they are aware of different aspects of Sam's job responsibilities, and since they may represent different levels of the organizational hierarchy.

There are different strategies for selecting raters:

- The subjects select the raters, choosing those people with whom they work on a regular basis. (Keep in mind that their list should be reviewed by someone who is familiar with their job, or they might conveniently leave off people who may give them negative feedback.)
- The subjects provide a list of suggested raters, selecting supervisors, peers, and subordinates. The list is then reviewed for additions or deletions by the Human Resouces/Personnel Department or a senior manager.
- The supervisor or Human Resources/Personnel selects the raters.
- Raters who work with the subject volunteer to evaluate.
- Some organizations provide a list of suggested raters and the subject gets to select from the list. This may allow the subject to eliminate someone who they feel will give them a particularly negative result. If it looks as though the negative rater will skew the rest of the results, this process may be a fair one.

The key to the selection of raters is to make sure that there is a distribution of coworkers who have a good idea of the work performance of the person they are about to evaluate.

11. WHAT IF THE RATER CANNOT WITNESS SOME OF THE BEHAVIORS?

The evaluation form should include all behaviors that are expected, but they should be behaviors that can actually be witnessed by coworkers.

For example, an organization may want all employees to focus on customers, but how often do the raters get to see actual employee-customer interaction? How can they evaluate an employee on a behavior that they never get a chance to witness? The work behaviors should be observable on a regular basis. Those who observe the behaviors can rate the subject. Those who do not have the opportunity should indicate "N/A" (not applicable) or "N/W" (not witnessed).

Of course, raters may not witness *all* work behaviors. They may observe the employee working in their department, but not in activities outside the department. For example, coworkers may not witness a salesperson interact with clients, but they do see office interaction, follow-up to client meetings, etc. Raters should not be expected to guess about some behaviors.

All forms should allow raters to indicate that a behavior is either not applicable (N/A) or simply not witnessed. Then raters do not find themselves giving a negative or false response just because they have not seen the behavior.

12. HOW CAN CONFIDENTIALLY BE GUARANTEED?

Confidentiality cannot be guaranteed. Every effort should be made to keep the process private and confidential, but people will still talk. Raters may compare notes with their colleagues and may talk to the subject about the process.

Raters may react with consternation if they feel that their handwriting can be traced, online assessments can be tracked, or codes on forms can be deciphered. If they have things to say that they feel are important for the company to know, they may not say them if they feel that they will be "discovered."

In addition, the subject often knows who is doing the evaluating, so the subject may try to figure out where the results came from. For example, if a subject is going to be evaluated by one supervisor, four peers, and three team members, it may not be hard to determine who said what. This can usually be settled by merging the data from several sources, making it difficult to determine isolated responses.

Strategies That Will Encourage Confidentiality Include:

- Do not require rater names, or code names, to be written on the evaluation forms.
- Distribute the forms to the raters in a private setting (not through personal mail or at a general meeting).
- Expect the forms to be completed at work.
- Stress the importance of professional treatment of the process.
- Establish a place for the forms to be completed (such as a conference room) so that they are not being filled out in a setting that has distractions, or conduct the process online with security measures.
- Establish one person who will oversee the distribution and collection of forms (someone who is well recognized for being discreet).
- Store the forms at a site that cannot be accessed by staff in general.
- Establish a data system that cannot be accessed by staff in general.
- Limit distribution of the results to the subject and the supervisor(s) who will be responsible for performance improvement.

13. WHAT FORMS SHOULD BE USED?

There are many evaluation forms available in software packages, in Human Resources literature, and on the Internet. The difficulty is selecting a form that will produce results that are actually useful.

Forms should be designed so that they are not very time-consuming and are accompanied by an opportunity for raters to add narrative notes that elaborate upon the numbers. A one-page form that has 25 questions (preferably with 1-4 rating) is usually quite sufficient as long as a second page is attached that allows for written comments.

The most important question to ask before selecting or creating a form is: What does the organization want to know? Select work behaviors and attitudes that are important to the company. Ask employees to help design the questions so that they can identify what they want to know for personal development, and so that they have an investment in the process. Tailor the forms for different jobs. Select items from job descriptions. Are the same behaviors and skills required from the heavy equipment operators as from the website developers? Should individuals in the Human Resources/Personnel Department be evaluated with the same criteria as the Sales Department personnel?

Some organizations may say that all employees should be evaluated on the same types of performance. Their jobs may be different, but they are all expected to be customer-focused, to possess strong communication skills, and to have excellent attendance records. They should be evaluated with the same criteria, across the board.

Other organizations may assess the same baseline skills across the board with all personnel, but may add specific expectations for different jobs. For example, the 360 criteria for executives may be different than the list of expected behaviors of frontline personnel. The final list of criteria depends upon what the organization values and what it wants to measure.

When selecting the content and format of the forms, it is also important to determine what the final results will look like, and how the results will be compiled for the subject.

14. WHAT DO 360 RESULTS LOOK LIKE?

The 360 assessment results are generally compiled into one report. Scores are averaged and written comments are typed up and attached. The results are more informative if the subject can see results overall, as well as results broken down by boss, peer, self, and team/employees. This way subjects can get very specific information about how they behave around different groups. They can also see how their self-perception compares to the perceptions of the other raters.

Some organizations prefer to have the subject's supervisor summarize the written comments verbally, so that raters will feel more comfortable writing comments. The raters can write specific details without worrying about whether they will be identified by the subject.

In more complex reports, the subject can see exactly how raters marked a particular skill. For example, the subject may see that five raters marked a "4" for presentation skills, and three raters marked a "3." If the report goes into further detail, the subject may see that the "4s" were all from peers, and the "3s" from bosses. The subject then discovers that "presentation skills" are perceived overall as very good with coworkers believing them to be excellent, but supervisors (or bosses) are still looking for some improvement. The narrative comments in the report may clarify what the supervisors are looking for, or the subject can discuss the results with a supervisor and create a related action plan.

The reports should be designed so that the results are clear and succinct and easy to interpret. If the subject spends more time trying to comprehend how to read the data than interpreting the results, the report is unnecessarily complex. The report should be presented so that comparisons between groups can be done quickly, written comments are tied to specific questions, and the content is arranged logically. (Before selecting a 360 vendor, it is important to check out the design of the final reports.)

Organizations can also get a general picture of the subjects as a group by combining all of the scores of all of the subjects. For example, if 17 managers participated in the 360, all of their scores can be averaged, and patterns of highs and lows of the entire group highlighted. The leadership of the organization may discover that more training is needed in customer service, or that the managers excel in speedy decision-making. This information can be used for organizational goal-setting and budgeting.

15. SHOULD A *SELF*-ASSESSMENT BE INCLUDED?

In most 360 assessments, the subject receives a report that has an average score for each behavior that has been evaluated. The boss, peer, and team scores are combined and averaged. If the results of the 360 consist of one combined rating from the boss, peers, and team, then the addition of "self" scores may lend confusion to the general picture. The "self" scores could skew the results. It would be hard to tell how personal perspectives align with the perspectives of coworkers because all of the scores are blended together.

However, if the results are broken out so that the subject can compare reactions from the different groups, it can be quite enlightening to compare results to the self scores. How do peers rate a work behavior as compared to the subject's rating of self? Does the boss agree with the self?

When self scores match other scores, the results can be encouraging. When subjects discover that their own self-perception is dramatically different than that of their colleagues, they will need to discuss these perceptions with their supervisor and analyze strategies for the future.

16. SHOULD CUSTOMERS BE INVOLVED IN THE 360?

Involve customers (external raters) if:

- They frequently interact with the subject and are very familiar with the job requirements and behaviors of the subject.
- They are comfortable that the process is fair and anonymous, and they are willing to participate.
- The customer feedback is valued as a reliable perspective.
- The customer feedback can influence individual behavior.
- The results are not used to determine overall customer satisfaction, but the customer's view of one individual's job-related behaviors.
- The customers have been well trained on the purpose and guidelines of the 360 process.
- Customer involvement in organizational procedures is routine.
- There is a desire to promote the organization's emphasis on customer feedback.

In addition to customers, other external contacts such as vendors, suppliers, and partner agencies can be valuable contributors to the 360 process.

17. HOW CAN 360s HELP AN ORGANIZATION?

360s can be used for employee and team development, formal performance appraisals, major organizational changes, and surgical improvements in the organization.

Obviously, the leaders of organizations desire to tap the talents, skills, and ideas of employees. When an organization implements a 360 assessment process, it sends the message that a thorough, fair evaluation is valued and that the organization will work to identify skills and will cultivate employee improvement. It sends the message that employee input is valued and that the organization strives to recognize employee strengths.

The organization gains improved communication, skill identification, and, hopefully, changed behaviors.

Employees generally think that they have a pretty good idea of how they are doing at work, but they can often be unaware of the impact of some of their behaviors on coworkers. If employees have been receiving regular feedback in informal dialogues and formal performance appraisals, then a 360 will provide more detailed information from a variety of sources about where the organization should spend time, money, and energy on improvements.

A 360 can give employees the opportunity to compare their personal view of their work behaviors with the views of their colleagues. Sometimes it is quite a surprise! For example, Ben thought that he was an organized and efficient supervisor. His 360 feedback showed that the employees he supervised all agreed with him. So did his boss. However, his fellow supervisors indicated in their 360 appraisals that he appeared to them to be disorganized, communicating mixed messages to different departments, and causing confusion. Ben immediately knew that he needed to focus on improving communication and planning with his fellow supervisors. If the organization had used a traditional performance appraisal system, limiting the process to just the boss and Ben, then Ben may not have known that there was a problem with the supervisors.

It helps to look at 360s as a process that will provide valuable information about:

- individual employees
- teamwork
- organizational climate
- customer service issues
- training needs
- mission alignment
- patterns of concern
- and problems that need to be addressed.

If administered efficiently and fairly, 360s can be a critical resource for organizational planning and decision-making.

Organizations may also wish to use the 360 in conjunction with employee surveys and customer service research, to get an overall picture of the status of the organization.

18. HOW CAN A 360 HELP EMPLOYEES?

If the 360 assessment is implemented, employees benefit in the following ways:

- Organizational expectations are clarified because the 360 forms specifically identify what the organization expects to witness.
- Results can reveal specific strengths and areas that need improvement, as perceived by identified groups (i.e., boss, peers, team/employees).
- Subjects can see if their self-perceptions are accurate.
- Results can be used as part of a progression plan and for identifying opportunities for advancement and other plans for the future.
- Results can answer the question "How am I doing?" without the need for supervisors to express the answer verbally to an employee, giving only one point of view.
- Results can be used for determining training needs or for reinforcing training requests.
- Results can be a useful intervention tool for supplementing coaching and for assisting a subject before discipline or termination may be necessary
- The 360 process can assist employees in expressing their observations and concerns in a confidential manner.
- Employees can feel invested in improving performance in an organization that recognizes the value of employee feedback.

19. WHAT IF THE 360 RESULTS ARE ALARMING?

The results of the 360 assessments should be reviewed as soon as possible because, on occasion, the results will reveal a significant problem with an employee, or with a department or team. Action should be taken immediately.

If the findings show behaviors that appear to be illegal, unethical, or in violation of company policy or procedures, then the Human Resources/Personnel Department may have to be involved in determining the appropriate steps to be taken. If the findings indicate that a subject needs immediate attention in the form of coaching or counseling, then intervention should be taken as quickly as possible by an appropriate, trained supervisor or Human Resources/Personnel specialist.

It is important for organizations to determine in advance how to handle problems that show up in the 360 results. These questions should be discussed prior to the implementation of the 360:

- *Who should be informed that there may be a problem?*
- *What steps will be followed to protect the rights of the employees while pursuing what is best for coworkers and the organization?*
- *How will the credibility and confidentiality of the 360 be maintained if intervention is taken that is obviously the result of the 360 assessment?*
- *How will the privacy of raters be protected?*

20. HOW CAN A 360 ENCOURAGE TEAMWORK?

Leaders of team-based organizations might assume that the 360 is a perfect way for members of teams to evaluate each other. Instead of using the full 360 process, just the team members evaluate each other. This process is often called a "peer review." It is not a true 360 because supervisors and other employees are usually not involved.

It takes exceptional employees in well established (often referred to as "fully functioning") teams to be able to comfortably evaluate their own team members. Peer review should be implemented only when there is already ongoing, open feedback about the performance of the individual team members and the team as an entire group. Even then it should be carried out only if the team members are comfortable with the process, and feel as if they can be candid and the results will be welcomed. Once again, the purpose of using a 360 for peer review should be for performance development.

For example, suppose that John is a member of a six-person engineering design team. The other five members evaluate his work behaviors, all using the same form. The results are given to him, summarized. He now knows what his team thinks of his work. What happens next? How blindsided will John be? Who will work with John on personal development? How will the results affect his level of comfort in working with the team in the future? John should be able to have an open discussion with the team to clarify concerns and to develop a plan of action.

The 360 process can be useful to Team Leaders who work closely with their teams but would appreciate more formal, objective feedback. Again, in a true team-based structure, there should be continuous opportunities for teams and their leaders to evaluate communication, goal achievement, customer service, production, quality, etc. When performance on the part of any employee, including the Team Leaders, needs improving, the team members (if the team is functioning well) should work together on skill development. The results of a 360 asessment of the Team Leader can be used for planning future team activities.

Some organizations have used the 360 format for team discussions about teamwork, rather than for formal evaluation of individuals. A facilitated discussion can allow for open evaluation of the strengths and weaknesses of the team, often revealing individual needs for training, coaching, or behavior modification.

The 360 process can also encourage teamwork if the subject gathers the raters together to share the action plan that was developed from the 360 results. By articulating personal goals, the subject invites the entire group to work as a team to assist the subject in personal development.

21. SHOULD A 360 BE USED WITH THE EXISTNG PERFORMANCE APPRAISAL SYSTEM?

A 360 can enhance a performance appraisal system by providing more detailed and tailored information. However, it can also be cumbersome to try to keep up-to-date on performance appraisals while carrying out a 360 assessment program. Both systems not only require the process of gathering information and completing paperwork (or electronic forms), but also require time to meet with employees to go over the results and create plans of action.

It is important for an organization to decide if the 360 will be the sole performance appraisal system, or whether it will supplement the existing appraisal system. If it will be used as the sole appraisal system, then employees must have the opportunity to respond to results and work together with supervisors to create a plan of action.

If the 360 is directly connected to compensation, the role of the raters changes. They are now determining the salaries of the subject. As one peer rater stated, "I can't fill this out honestly because I don't want to be responsible for someone's paycheck." Since 360s are recommended as developmental tools, they are not always as effective if raises are linked to results. Employees may resent the fact that their future depends upon their colleagues, and not on their boss, because they are used to working to please their supervisors.

In some cases, a 360 is administered after a performance appraisal, when an employee desires to know more about his or her work performance, or when the organization needs a way to gather feedback from a variety of sources so that it can create a broader picture of employee performance.

A 360 can also be used in conjunction with employee and customer satisfaction surveys, employee feedback sessions, and so forth, in order to obtain a general sense of organizational success and skill areas that require improvement.

22. CAN 360S BE USED IN A UNION ENVIRONMENT?

The relationship between management and labor will be a major influence on the success of a new appraisal process such as the 360 assessment. Past history, the style and credibility of management and union leadership, and the status of negotiations will all be major factors in determining whether the 360 can be implemented effectively.

In some cases, the method of appraisal is specified in labor agreements and contracts. If the organization includes union groups, it is important to:

• Review labor-management agreements to determine the processes of appraisal, the steps for changing appraisal methods, the level of involvement of union representatives in appraisal systems, and grievance procedures tied to employee appraisals.

• Involve union representatives in designing and implementing the 360 process, establishing the parameters of union/management deci- sion- making before beginning the process.

• Review the grievance procedure process with the 360 assessment in mind, recognizing that more than two people (supervisor and employee) will be involved in the assessment process. How will dis- agreements about the 360 results be settled? Who will be involved in mediating? What will be the procedure and time frame for filing com- plaints?

• Recognize that seniority, gain-sharing, promotions, job assign- ments, and access to skill-training are often union-based concerns and should be considered when determining how to use the results of the 360s.

23. HOW CAN A 360 CULTIVATE A GOOD RELATIONSHIP WITH THE BOSS?

It depends upon the boss.

It also depends on the receptivity of the subject.

The 360 process can be conducted quite smoothly and then com- pletely fall apart when it comes time for the subject to discuss the results with the supervisor.

If the supervisor uses the 360 as an excuse to criticize and demand, then the purpose of the 360 as a developmental tool is lost. On the other hand, if the subject insists on debating and rejecting the 360 results, then the purpose of gathering multiple perspectives is lost.

The 360 can be an excellent tool for cultivating good boss–subject relationships if the boss:

- understands the purpose of the 360 as a developmental tool
- completes training in how to conduct a performance assessment meeting
- reads and highlights the appraisal results
- identifies strong areas that should be encouraged and praised
- identifies areas of development that can only be clarified with a thorough discussion
- recognizes that scores that are "outliers" may be significant because they represent the truth, or because they represent a

biased rater. (Individual score results, as well as total results, should be discussed with the subject.)

- conducts an open discussion that involves more listening than talking
- comes to agreement with the subject about skill areas that should be maintained and skill areas that need attention
- specifies action plan objectives, and is willing to provide resources to assist the subject in improving behaviors.

The subject's primary responsibility is to be willing to learn. An open-minded subject should study the 360 results, weigh the findings and think about the context and the messages, prepare for a plan-oriented session with the supervisor, and follow through. This is helpful to the subject, and will probably impress the boss!

24. WHAT ARE THE WORST REASONS FOR IMPLEMENTING A 360?

The 360 assessment process should not be used to:

- build documentation on one individual solely for discipline or termination
- identify targets for downsizing
- gather data without providing follow-up or support for subjects
- stockpile ammunition.

The 360 is to help employees, not punish them.

25. HOW CAN THE PAPERWORK BE REDUCED WHEN IMPLEMENTING A 360?

A 360 process can involve a lot of paper. The most efficient means of conducting a 360 is to do it online because it reduces the time involved in gathering and collecting, and with some programs, the results can be collated and summarized.

If the forms must be completed manually, consider these tips:

• Keep the forms simple, short, and to the point.
• Select small groups to be assessed, conducting periodic 360s.
• Establish one person to collect and file information at one collection point.
• Set up a collection system that allows for immediate filing of completed forms (in the subject's 360 file).
• Color code the boss, self, peer, and team forms.

26. SHOULD A 360 BE COMPLETED ELECTRONICALLY?

Electronic 360 assessments are an efficient substitute for paper and pencil methods. Software programs or online assessments, available from businesses (often found on the Internet), can provide:

• assistance in developing forms
• electronic distribution and collection
• e-mail instruction, reminders, and time frames
• data security
• data compilation and summarizing
• highlight of areas of development and training
• links to learning resources
• identification of trends, strong areas of performance, historical patterns, goal-setting guides, and action plan outlines
• continuous tips.

("Key Words" for tracking down 360 programs on the Internet include: *performance review, 360 degree, assessment, evaluation, employee development,* and *feedback tools.*)

Raters can complete 360 assessment forms online, but will only feel comfortable with the process if they believe that it is confidential. Electronic collection of data can be speedy, especially if time frames for completion are clear. For example, one company alerted raters that the forms would be e-mailed for a 1:00 p.m. appointment, with the understanding that the 360s would be completed privately online at that time.

Electronic completion can get complicated if an employee is filling out forms for several different coworkers. For example, a supervisor may be completing several assessments on fellow supervisors, while completing forms on senior managers and employees. It is essential to look closely at the availability of the forms, the timing of their completion and, of course, the possibility of technological "glitches."

Another electronic alternative is the interactive voice response system (IVR), which allows raters the opportunity to answer a series of questions on the phone. The IVR system collates the data. Although this process allows for quick completion, it does not necessarily allow raters time to think about their responses and to look over the entire assessment when they are done. Although raters should not be encouraged to change their initial responses, quite often rater's will review their assessments to make sure that they gave fair and accurate pictures of their perceptions of the subject's work behaviors. In reflection, some answers may have to be changed. The IVR allows for speed of form completion and immediacy of results, but does not allow raters extra time to contemplate responses.

27. WHO OWNS THE RESULTS?

Before implementing a 360°-assessment process, determine where the final copies will be housed, who will have access to the files, how long they will be retained, and how long they will remain confidential and secure

Determine if participation in the process is *required*, including whether subjects must develop action plans that identify areas of personal development. What if a rater refuses to complete a form because they do not want a written record of their evaluation of a boss or coworker (even if it is done anonymously)?

Some organizations keep the results in individualized personnel files, treating the final copies as a formal appraisal, owned by the organization (with a copy to the subject). If the organization requests that the 360 be signed by the subject, it is important to determine if signing the copy indicates simply that it has been read, or whether the subject has read it and agrees with the contents.

Since the 360 results are meant to serve as a resource for creating a plan for personal development, it is a good idea to discuss the results and create an action plan that is signed by the subject and supervisor. The actual 360 report would then belong to the subject.

Chapter 6

THE TRUTH ABOUT DELEGATION

Why did you cringe when I said the word "delegation"?
(Business Manager, suggesting that a supervisor delegate a project to an employee.)

When supervisors delegate effectively, they release an important task to a trusted employee. They delegate because the task needs to be completed and the selected employee will benefit from being responsible for getting it accomplished.

When supervisors delegate, they match a task to an employee who is ready for a challenge and can handle the responsibility. Who would be interested in tackling this project? Who has the unique skills necessary to get this done? Who needs to expand contacts and build visibility? Who wants to learn something new?

When supervisors delegate, they clearly describe the objectives of the task, the time frame, resources and support systems that are available, and the benefits to the selected employee. They do *not* specify how the task will be organized and carried out, and they do *not* expect to provide final approval for every step. When supervisors delegate, they provide direction and initial suggestions and guidance. Then, on occasion, they check in with the employee to assess progress. The employee has full responsibility for determining the best approach to the task, the actions and resources necessary to carry it out, and the system for monitoring progress.

Delegation can be a difficult dance sometimes, as supervisors want to empower employees to take charge, but do not want to completely abdicate responsibility. After all, the supervisors may be held accountable if the task is not accomplished properly.

This chapter describes how the delegation process is supposed to work, and how supervisors can delegate so that they feel secure in the process and the employees feel honored and respected for being selected.

1. WHAT IS DELEGATION?

Supervisors who delegate are *entrusting* employees with *important* tasks, and giving them *authority* with *responsibility.* Delegation usually involves deferring a supervisory task to an employee. The supervisor still has the ultimate accountability for the task, but the employee is trusted to plan and carry out the activities related to the task.

Although many supervisors do not realize it, delegation is the quintessential supervisory skill. If supervisors can delegate successfully, it is a sign that they are organized and can comfortably coordinate work. They can communicate clearly with employees, establish a free flow of information, and maintain positive relationships with their employees. Supervisors who delegate recognize that they can become overloaded and bogged down, and that delegation of some of the workload can ease the pressure and can allow employees to develop and shine.

It is not easy to include delegation in daily management strategies. Delegation takes skill and effort, and is often misunderstood.

To gain a better picture of delegation, imagine that you are a sheriff in a small town in the 1800s. You have to catch some "bad guys" who just robbed your only bank. As the townspeople gather in front of your jail, you survey the crowd and begin to think about selecting your deputies.

You realize that you cannot ride off on your own and expect to catch the entire gang single-handedly, and you are also concerned about leaving the town vulnerable when you are gone. Even though you are in charge, you cannot be everywhere at once, and you cannot take on every single task. You need help.

(Prepare to delegate!)

You know what needs to be done and you know how to achieve your goal. You have had experience with catching bank robbers before (after all, that is why they made you the sheriff), and you have developed some good systems for getting criminals captured.

You explain your plan to the crowd, listen to their suggestions, and then announce that you will need to select some deputies to assist in the chase. The crowd stands at attention, wary about who you may choose. Each townsperson would like to help protect the town, and may even look forward to an adventure. But they all have mixed emotions. Shouldn't the *sheriff* be catching the bank robbers? (After all, that is why they made you sheriff, correct?) Don't they already have enough to do? How will they be compensated? What if they have never done this before, and what if they fail? Who is responsible if the robbers get away?

You, as the sheriff, understand the crowd's concerns, but also see that the job needs to be done with help from the townspeople. It is a big responsibility, and the sheriff's role will be to provide clear instructions about goals, activities, and deadlines.

Some of the townspeople need a challenge, a chance to enhance their skills or learn something new. Some have expressed their desire to experience something different than their normal responsibilities.

The task of pursuing the bank robbers may be a difficult one, and may require some juggling and reprioritizing, but you know that with some guidance there are townspeople who can get the job done. You need to select those townspeople who can make a strong contribution, can figure out how to adjust their workload to accommodate this new responsibility, and can approach a new task as a challenge and not as a burden. Once these characteristics are taken into consideration, it starts to become clear who should be deputized. (Time to delegate!)

Your first choice is the blacksmith who is well known for his tracking skills. He has assisted in posses before, and knows how to meet a challenge under pressure. He has the right combination of related skills and the ability to take on a difficult job.

Your second choice is the storekeeper. She grew up in the town and has explored the countryside all of her life. She is a natural organizer and, although her store keeps her busy, she wants to expand her horizons. She is the right person to tackle something new while applying her expertise.

For your third deputy you decide to choose the teller who can recognize the robbers. He is fairly new at his job, but he has had some Pinkerton training, and is anxious to become a contributing member to the community. He may be uncertain at first, but he has a valuable background that needs to be developed further.

Once you deputize your charges, you explain the goal: *Bring back the robbers alive.* You will stay in town to maintain protection and to follow up on the robbery, and will then meet the deputies at sunset at Castle Rock to check on progress.

You then pass along some guidelines and advice, and make sure that the deputies are fully equipped for the job.

So far your delegation strategies have been to:

- identify a challenging task
- consider who might be interested in the task
- select who can handle the task
- clarify the goal and activities
- explain the role of the sheriff
- share advice
- establish parameters of the job
- provide resources
- make arrangements to meet.

As you delegate this significant task to your deputies, you make it clear that you want to tap their skills and cultivate their potential, and that you trust that they can handle the job without constant supervision. They seem a little nervous, so you provide encouragement and suggestions. You advise them to plan together and set up a means of communicating, and you explain the limits to their authority. They are to keep you informed, but they can get the job done in their own way. You may share tips from your own experience, but you recognize that they will probably carry out the task differently than the way that you would do it.

When you meet your deputies at Castle Rock at the end of the day you hear what they have to say, share a few thoughts of your own, and plan the next steps together. If you have any concerns, you do some coaching and provide more detailed direction.

Then the deputies are on their own once again. You are still monitoring the project and still setting the parameters, but you have *faith* that the deputies you selected will figure out the best way to achieve the goal. As a result, the deputies should feel *honored* that they have been selected.

Your delegation strategies have now included:

- providing further direction
- working together to solve problems

- clarifying limits
- encouraging and supporting
- refraining from dictating style and approach
- communicating on a regular basis.

As shown by this sheriff example, it is clear that delegation involves *entrusting* important tasks to individuals who can handle the challenge and need the opportunity to take on something new. Supervisors may release the tasks, but there is still oversight to make sure that the tasks are on track and the goals are achieved. The deputies (those who have been selected to take on a delegated task), get to develop their skills, build credibility and trust, and add to their list of accomplishments.

It is hard to think of delegation in terms of *trust, faith,* and *honor.* But excellent supervisors employ delegation as a means of sharing important components of the workload while encouraging employees to build knowledge, experience, and confidence.

2. WHAT IS *NOT* DELEGATION?

The process of delegating is often misunderstood by supervisors.

Delegation is not passing along work that is unappealing to the supervisor and the employees.

Supervisors who delegate effectively understand that the tasks that are handed over to employees are selected because they will enhance employee skills, provide new challenges, or allow exposure to new contacts and fields of expertise. They should not be tasks that are tedious or routine, or tasks that the supervisor just does not feel like doing.

Delegation is not dumping work that is time-consuming.

Supervisors who delegate effectively understand that when they are feeling overwhelmed and suddenly "delegate" some of their "to do" list to employees, they are really "dumping" work, often to employees who are already very busy. Delegated work should help employees to expand skills and assume greater responsibilities, not just ease the workload of the supervisors.

Delegation is not abdicating supervisory responsibilities.

Supervisors who delegate effectively understand that there are tasks that should be solely the responsibility of the supervisor if they involve unique supervisory expertise, limited authority, confidentiality, or difficult decisions requiring an organizational perspective. Supervisors should not delegate tasks because they do not want to "take the heat" or want to avoid conflict.

Delegation is not quick assignments to fill gaps.

Supervisors who delegate effectively understand that when an employee's work level has slowed down or an employee appears to be able to temporarily help out with tasks, the quick, short-term assignments are *not* "delegated" tasks. A delegated task is usually a project or activity that requires the employee to plan, set up a system, and then follow through.

It is clear that true delegation has *not* taken place when the following is in evidence:

- Supervisors dictate the process to be used, requiring the employee to carry out the task the same way the supervisor would.
- The employee resents the added work without understanding the benefits of the delegated task, or without gaining the promised benefits.
- The employee is given little guidance, assistance, or resources to fulfill the delegated task.
- The delegated task is part of everyday, routine work life and is not something challenging to the employee.
- The supervisor shifts a heavy assignment to an employee without discussing the impact on the employee's workload.
- The supervisor who delegated the tasks takes the credit for a job well done.

Is This Supervisor Delegating?

1. Mark (a supervisor) was in the middle of preparing a budget when he was called to a meeting. He asked Ted (because Ted is good with numbers) to finish calculating the totals for each budget category, while Mark attended the meeting. Is this delegation?

2. Susan (a supervisor) decided that the Customer Service Center should be more cheerful, but she knew that she did not have the skills to decorate effectively. She asked Jeff and Mary, who were both artistic, to decorate colorful, attractive bulletin boards for the end of each hall. Is this delegation?

3. George (a supervisor) suspected that one of his employees (Jack) was emotionally depressed, but did not know how to talk to him about it. He asked Jerry, one of Jack's coworkers, to meet with Jack to discuss counseling available through the Employee Assistance Program. Is this delegation?

4. Elizabeth (a supervisor) was responsible for keeping up-to-date about services offered by similar businesses in her geographical area. She had difficulty finding time to do this, so she asked Carol (who was a seasoned employee and *very* organized) to keep tabs on services, to keep her informed, and to provide her with flyers, handouts, mailings, etc. from other businesses. Is this delegation?

5. John (a supervisor) was about to go on vacation when he realized that he could not complete his inventory by the end of the day. He noticed that Marcia seemed to be ahead of her daily schedule, so he assigned her one of the storage rooms to inventory. Is this delegation?

6. Kevin (a supervisor) felt that Kate was ready for more responsibility, so he asked her to monitor the quality of her coworker's record-keeping and then report sloppy records to him. Is this delegation?

7. Ellen told Brian, her secretary, to make her a cup of coffee. Is this delegation?

Answer: The only true task that can be called delegation is 4. The delegated assignment allows Carol to expand her knowledge base and become more valuable to the organization. Elizabeth is a manager who recognizes her personal time limitations and is confident enough to release this important task to a trusted employee.

Tasks 1 and 2 are routine sharing of the workload, or may even be "dumping" work.

Under most circumstances 3, 6, and 7 are inappropriate assignments for employees. Jeff and Mary, described in #2, may be honored by

Susan's request, but only if the project seems essential to the organization, and is intriguing to Jeff and Mary. It may be an appropriate request, but should not be called "delegation."

3. WHY SHOULD SUPERVISORS DELEGATE?

Supervisors who successfully delegate have discovered that delegation is an indication of a confident, well-organized, and considerate leader. Those who struggle with delegation tend to think of it as a weakness because they think that it looks as if they cannot handle their workload. Once the first delegated task is completed effectively, supervisors who were nervous about delegating discover the following rewards from delegation:

• Employees feel respected and trusted, resulting in higher morale and productivity.

• The supervisor is regarded with respect, as someone who recognizes and encourages employees (and is not threatened by talent around them).

• Supervisors get credit for knowing employees well, making good matches of employees to tasks, and supporting valuable contributors to the organization.

• Employees build skills that are not only in new areas of expertise, but in organization, planning, and communication.

• Supervisors learn about new and perhaps better ways of getting things done.

• Employees can become the resident expert on a topic, providing information to the supervisor (who does not have time to keep up on all topics), and increasing their own value to the organization.

• Supervisors can reduce their workload by releasing important tasks to employees they trust.

• Employees can "spread their wings" while knowing that the supervisor will continue to provide support and direction.

4. WHY WON'T SUPERVISORS DELEGATE?

When supervisors are asked why they do not delegate, they can usually come up with lots of explanations. The primary reason, however, seems to be that they believe that it is simply "easier to just do it myself."

This may be true. If the task can be done efficiently by the supervisor and there is a guarantee that the supervisor can do it the very best way—then the task should not be delegated. If, however, the supervisor cannot find time to do it right and could use some assistance, then perhaps it is worth it to delegate the task. The amount of time monitoring delegation is certainly less than the amount of time it takes to "do it myself."

What are some of the reasons given by supervisors when they do not delegate?

Fear Of Letting Go

- What if the employee does a better job?
- What if it looks as though I could not handle the workload?
- What if I delegate and it all falls apart?

Delegation is especially difficult for supervisors who achieved their position because they have a unique specialization and are known for their area of expertise. Once those supervisors realize that both supervisors and employees benefit from delegation, the process becomes routine.

Delegating Ends Up To Be More Work

- What if the employee falls behind or makes mistakes?
- What if the employee is clearly overwhelmed?

Supervisors who understand delegation realize that constant communication with the employee is still essential, even if the employee has been given full responsibility for a delegated task.

The Supervisor Desires To Do It "My Way"

Supervisors may believe that their style, their system, or their process is the *only* way. The key to successful delegation is recognizing that the goals of the supervisors and employees should be the same, but the approach that the employees take may be very different than the approach of the supervisors.

Unreliable/Inexperienced Staff

Smaller organizations may have a limited number of employees who can take on a delegated task. But small, unique tasks can be delegated for the purpose of building employee skills and reducing the pressure on supervisors. There is value in cross-training so that employees will have multiple areas of expertise, especially in a small organization. When hiring, look for individuals who express true interest in learning a variety of skills.

Confusion About Supervisory Role

Too many supervisors believe that once they move up in the ranks they have to justify their title by taking on every single task. But strong supervisors recognize that knowing all of the answers and being available at all times does not necessarily constitute effective leadership. In fact, good supervisors work closely with employees to help them to build their skills and self-reliance. A *strong supervisor* knows that building a *strong staff* makes everyone a better worker.

Martyr Complex

Some supervisors may want to make it clear that they are so very, very important because they have so much work to do! A harried supervisor with an overloaded briefcase does not represent important power and responsibiity, but poor organization and time management, and perhaps an unwillingness to delegate. Supervisors who constantly express frustration with their workload can be viewed as leaders who want to have their importance acknowledged and who do not value the contributions of employees. Supervisors who delegate are respected for their understanding that employees and supevisors can both benefit from delegation.

Employees Are Swamped

Some supervisors feel that by sharing the workload, they are making employees stressed and overworked. If accommodations in the work schedule are difficult to make, discuss how the delegated task can be accomplished. How will priorities change? What can be eliminated? Who can provide assistance? What resources will facilitate achieving the goal? Keep in mind that delegation does mean additional tasks, but the experience builds skills and value to the organization.

5. WHAT ARE THE CLUES THAT IT IS TIME TO DELEGATE?

Usually supervisors can tell it is time to delegate when they see an item constantly resurfacing on their calendar and it still has not been addressed. Or it may be time to delegate when a new task emerges that is the perfect chance for employee development. When a supervisor thinks, "Who needs the opportunity to tackle this so it will get done well and on time?" then the supervisor is thinking like a delegator. Examples of clues that it is time to delegate include:

- An employee expresses the desire to try something new.
- A big project is looming and keeps getting postponed.
- More knowledge is needed on a specific subject.
- A section of a project needs more attention and no one is really in charge of it.
- New ideas, new energy are needed for a task.
- A specific issue keeps ending up on the back burner, but at some point needs to be addressed.
- A procedure needs to be improved by someone who has experience.

6. WHAT SHOULD SUPERVISORS DELEGATE?

Supervisors should delegate tasks that are the overall responsibility of one person or a team of persons, with the understanding that other employees may get involved as the work gets under way. When a task is delegated, it is assumed that the responsible employee will consult with coworkers, conduct appropriate research, and perhaps establish a committee to assist in achieving the goals.

Tasks that fall in the following categories are usually appropriate for delegation:

Short-Term Projects

Example: Survey employees and analyze results
Example: Research available technology for a new service
Example: Benchmark product testing

New Areas Of Expertise

Example: Review new legislation that affects policy development
Example: Maintain up-to-date knowledge about research findings in a specific field
Example: Organize and conduct training in an area of specialization

Revision Of Procedure

Example: Improve health and safety outcomes with a new piece of equipment
Example: Decrease error rate on a standardized form
Example: Assess customer reception and revise protocols

Reorganization Of A Department Or Division

Example: Oversee office relocation
Example: Consult with staff about design of possible organizational charts
Example: Research similar job titles and responsibilities in the same field of work

Creative Approaches

Example: Design a customer-friendly reception area
Example: Organize a conference that will attract new participants
Example: Plan staff meetings so that attendance improves

Additional examples of delegated tasks that are usually the responsibility of a supervisor, but can be natural extensions of an employee's job and useful to the employer and the organization are:

- tracking trends and fads
- organizing hiring and interviewing
- learning technological skills such as website development
- public speaking at conferences and community events
- developing budget projections
- assisting in website development
- creating publications such as newsletters, brochures, and educational materials
- applying for grants
- representing the organization at fund-raisers and ceremonies
- visiting organizations to gather ideas about systems, software, teambuilding, etc.
- contacting vendors and suggesting purchases.

As long as the task has been initially assigned to the supervisor, is intriguing to the employee, and will have valuable results for the organization, then the supervisor should consider the possibility of delegation.

7. TO WHOM SHOULD A SUPERVISOR DELEGATE?

Supervisors generally delegate to one person, but occasionally it is necessary to select a small group to carry out a task. Choosing the right person(s) when delegating is certainly specific to the organization, but once a manager has a task in mind, the following *employee characteristics* should be considered:

- willing to try something different
- strong past history in following through
- need for something new and stimulating
- expressed interest in related tasks, and/or some degree of experience in the field
- interest in advancement, exposure to new contacts
- ability to work independently (or to work with a selected group)
- ability to accept guidance and direction
- ability to gather ideas and information comfortably
- manages time well, organized

- good interpersonal skills, generally good relationships with colleagues
- needs opportunity to "shine"
- expressed desire during performance appraisals to "expand horizons."

There are, of course, many other qualities that can be considered, but the supervisor who knows the employees fairly well can make the best selection. Supervisors may select an employee because of strong skills in the task area, or may select an employee who desires to learn about the task area for the first time. An employee may be chosen because the senior management recognizes potential, or because a supervisor believes in an employee who may have gone unrecognized. Most important is that the manager delegate fairly, being careful not to choose the same employees over and over again, and to avoid making selections on the basis of personal friendship or employee visibility.

8. HOW DO EMPLOYEES BENEFIT FROM DELEGATION?

It may not always feel like an "honor" to be delegated a task. Selected employees may regard the new task as an unwanted addition to the workload, creating stress and longer hours. Supervisors should match the task and the employee carefully, and should make it clear that the selected employee can benefit in the following ways:

- Credit and recognition will be given to the employee when work is carried out successfully.
- Time management of all work assignments, including the delegated task, will be addressed. If necessary, priorities will change and expectations reevaluated.
- The employee will be able to expand contacts, areas of knowledge, and skills. Delegation is a résumé builder and can result in positive feedback on performance appraisals.
- Delegation can provide a much-needed diversion from tasks that have become routine.
- Delegation implies "trust." The supervisor recognized the positive characteristics of the employee and chose carefully.

- Guidance, support, direction, and resources will be readily available. The supervisor will expect the employee to "check in" often.
- The employee will have the freedom to design and implement personal systems of carrying out the tasks, as long as the goals and timelines are being met.

Supervisors should follow through on these promised benefits.

9. WHAT ARE THE STEPS TO DELEGATION?

If delegation is done properly, with a true understanding of the definition and benefits, then the supervisor should always follow these steps:

1. Select the task.
2. Determine the best employee for the task.
3. Consider the benefits to the employee.
4. Consider the benefits to the organization.
5. Explain the task to the employee.

- Be specific about the purpose and the goals, making it clear that the employee can determine the process.
- Explain the supervisor's role in providing resources and contacts.
- Explain the need for the supervisor to check on the status of the assignment so that progress is steady.
- Give the employee time to think about the task and return with questions and requests. (Clarify ahead of time if the employee can turn down the request.)
- Immediately provide space, materials, e-mail addresses, and other forms of assistance that can facilitate completion of the task.
- Go ahead and share thoughts on how the task might be accomplished, but stress that the employee can figure out the best system.

6. Be clear about accountability and credit.

- Specify a schedule for regular updates, expectations for progress, timeline, highlights, etc.

- Determine how progress will be credited publicly and privately with the employee.
- Be clear about what will be done if the employee is struggling. (How will help be provided?)
- Be clear about what will be done if the employee is failing to complete the task.

7. Alert other employees about the employee's new task and how the delegation will be handled.

8. Meet regularly, informally and formally.

- Do not lose track of the timeline.
- Do not delegate and forget.

9. Open the door.

- Make it clear that delegation is viewed as an opportunity for employees to learn.
- If they are confused and frustrated, or pleased and proud, the supervisor should know about it.

10. Include the results in the employee's performance appraisal.

- Write up successes in newsletters, make announcements, provide rewards, circulate final reports, and advertise the employee's new area of expertise.
- Include formal documentation in the personnel file.

10. WHAT ARE THE OBSTACLES TO SUCCESSFUL DELEGATION?

Barriers to successful delegation can be created by supervisors. Some of the obstacles created by supervisors are:

- attempting to "sell" a delegated task when it is clear that the task is actually unappealing work that the supervisor is avoiding
- delegating a task to an employee when it is actually the responsibility of a coworker who had failed to follow through

- delegating a task that the supervisor does not have time to finish (and the deadline is soon)
- promising to provide resources and assistance, but failing to follow through
- delegating a task that requires resources that are unavailable (e.g., budget, support staff, travel, etc.) or an unreasonable time frame
- insisting on dictating the process (i.e., telling the employee to carry out the task the same way that the manager would do it)
- allowing the employee to discover office politics, hidden agendas, and other barriers without warning or assistance in successfully handling potential obstacles
- delegating a task that requires the unique expertise of outside vendors
- delegating a task that involves coaching or counseling a coworker –or monitoring the work of a coworker
- selecting an employee without considering whether it is a good match of employee to task
- failing to provide recognition and credit for carrying out the task.

Supervisors who have seriously considered the definition of *delegation*, have carefully selected the task and the employee, and have followed the steps to delegation, should be able to avoid running into obstacles as they delegate. As employees adjust to their new responsibility, often balancing a number of tasks and facing new hurdles, supervisors must be readily available to provide guidance and encouragement.

---

11. WHAT ARE THE SIGNS THAT DELEGATION IS NOT WORKING?

Supervisors should watch for warning signs that the delegation process may be in trouble. Employees may be:

- avoiding reporting, indicating that progress is slow or the news is not very good
- reporting too often, requiring specific direction rather than feedback

- spending time "getting organized," "setting-up," or "planning the process," rather than carrying out the task
- neglecting other responsibilities
- imposing work on others (or demanding their time, resources, or staff)
- flaunting authority in regard to a task
- on the wrong track because the task was misunderstood or the employee was unfamiliar with how to carry it out
- on the wrong track because the employee's work habits or interpersonal skills are weak.

In most cases, when there are clues that delegation is not working, supervisors can step in and get the employee back on track.

But there is always the possibility that the wrong person was selected, the task was too difficult, or the supervisor did not follow the delegation process.

If an employee expresses concern that the job is too overwhelming, or there are strong clues that delegation is not working, the supervisor has two choices:

1. Intervene and review the task, making changes in the size or focus of the task, or improving on the delegation process.
2. Take the task back.

Delegation, once administered, is not final. If it is not working, and the supervisor feels that sufficient guidance has taken place, then the delegation should be brought to a halt. If the work of the employee has been continuously monitored and regular assistance provided, the supervisor should be able to stop the decline before damage has been done.

12. WHAT ARE THE CHARACTERISTICS OF A SUCCESSFUL DELEGATOR?

Supervisors should be successful at delegation if they exhibit the following characteristics:

- always assessing employees to determine who could benefit from delegation
- releasing significant tasks so that employees can gain experience and recognition
- delegating instead of falling behind, postponing, and working longer hours
- adjusting workloads so that employees can comfortably assume delegated tasks
- providing guidance and resources, rather than specific direction
- maintaining accessibility when employees need guidance
- stepping *back* and letting employees devise their own systems
- stepping *in* to provide support and advice if the employee is getting off track or struggling
- stepping *up* to "take the heat" if senior management does not understand delegation of a task or how a task is being carried out
- providing recognition and rewards for a job well done.

Chapter 7

THE TRUTH ABOUT REWARDS
AND RECOGNITION

I would like to thank you all for your perseverance and creativity.
(Technology Supervisor at a pizza party celebration at the end of a big project.)

Employees appreciate praise. Even those employees who willingly work hard because they have a strong work ethic, or love what they do, or are simply thankful to have a paycheck, appreciate positive reinforcement. They respect those supervisors who make the effort to compliment and thank employees. They welcome the occasional reward for hard work, whether it is in the form of a certificate for the office wall, free passes to the movies, public recognition, or an incentive bonus.

Rewards and recognition can motivate employees to achieve goals, maximize their skills, and try new approaches to problems. In some cases, employees will work towards achieving a specific reward offered by the organization. In other cases, the employees may maintain quality work because they have been recognized for their achievements and wish to "keep up the good work." Either way, the employees feel appreciated for their contributions and are encouraged to be productive, safe, creative, and cost-efficient.

But what if the organization cannot afford to reward employees beyond their salaries? What if the employees have low morale or are difficult to motivate? What happens if the employees think that the recognition process is unfair, or what if supervisors do not know how to identify the employees who should be rewarded?

Supervisors can continuously acknowledge the accomplishments of employees as a routine part of their job. They do not need a formal rewards and recognition system in order to motivate and praise

168

employees. However, organizations that establish structured rewards and recognition systems that are carefully thought out and strategically implemented see increased productivity, higher job satisfaction, and loyalty to the organization.

This chapter describes the purposes and variables of rewards and recognition systems, steps to implementation, and inexpensive strategies.

1. WHAT ARE REWARDS AND RECOGNITION?

Recent literature related to the motivation of employees has stressed the importance of *rewards* and *recognition.*

Rewards in the workplace are usually defined as tangible items that are given to employees for a job well done. Rewards generally have a monetary value, and are often in the form of gift certificates, prizes, bonuses, and promotions or pay increases.

Recognition in the workplace usually involves public praise that calls attention to the excellent work of employees. Recognition may come with a *reward,* but it generally involves celebrating accomplishments with such things as certificates, newsletter articles, posted pictures, and announcements at staff meetings. Occasionally, recognition is more personalized, such as a thank-you e-mail message, a private verbal compliment, or a surprise meeting with senior management.

Rewards and recognition occur when an employee, team, unit, department, or branch of a business makes an important contribution to the success of the organization. The contribution could be a major effort such as managing a project, organizing a conference, or repairing vital equipment. Although big accomplishments may be visible and attract attention, rewards and recognition are a means of formally acknowledging and thanking employees for obvious achievements.

Quieter accomplishments that have positively impacted the success of the organization can also be recognized, such as resolving a customer complaint or streamlining a shipping process. On the surface, the task may appear to be minor, but the efforts of the employees may have saved the organization time and money, and may have contributed to better teamwork, reduced stress, and higher morale.

Rewards and recognition may also involve investment in employees who have earned special treatment. The organization may pay for

attendance at a conference, organize a luncheon that honors employees, or conduct a social event that is designed expressly to thank an
entire staff.

Those employees who make either subtle or dramatic contributions
are demonstrating the qualities of hard-working, dedicated employees.
Rewards and recognition may not be necessary to call attention to
their hard work, but the attention is usually appreciated. Rewards and
recognition can serve to motivate employees to seek out ways to
improve processes and to achieve organizational goals.

2. SHOULD EMPLOYEES BE RECOGNIZED AND REWARDED?

Are rewards and recognition really worth the time and expense?
Shouldn't employees have the work ethic to do an excellent job for the
paycheck? Do employees actually appreciate the special attention?

Skeptics say that recognition sets up competition among employees,
causing teamwork and productivity to falter. They believe that it is too
difficult to identify specific "winners," and that employees may fail to
identify problems, for fear of jeopardizing possible rewards.

Some employees resent the distribution of rewards and recognition
because they see the process as inequitable, based on luck, and
designed to ignore those employees who always do consistently outstanding work because it is simply their job to do so. Employees may
also see rewards and recognition as hypocritical if the climate of the
organization is normally oppressive and uncomfortable.

These concerns are legitimate, so it is important to look at the *context* of rewards and recognition. Employees respond positively to
recognition activities if the work environment is already comfortable,
or problems in the work environment are at least being addressed.
Employees also respond positively if there are visible efforts at being
fair in the distribution of rewards, and if the recognition is sincere, and
not in direct contrast to normal treatment. Employees also respond
enthusiastically to recognition if it is thoughtful and appropriate.

Employees who earn rewards and recognition feel positive about
making a successful contribution to the organization. They feel more
confident and are inspired to repeat what they did well.

For example, if Julie is complimented in front of her colleagues for
the style in which she handles difficult customers, Julie not only feels

proud of herself, but will also want to maintain the recognized behavior. If Dennis is awarded a surprise gift certificate for solving a serious problem while working a night shift, he appreciates that managers noticed, and that they bothered to acknowledge his achievement. He will probably approach the next problem with confidence and renewed dedication.

Many employees will state that they do not need to be recognized. In fact, they may say that they find it silly and embarrassing. They may believe that they are being paid sufficiently and whatever they accomplish is simply part of the job. Those employees may not enjoy the public attention and may be confused about why incentives are even necessary. They may not need (or desire) public recognition, but would more than likely still appreciate personalized attention. It encourages employees when they know that their personnel file contains a special letter, their boss personally and privately acknowledges their hard work, or their family can enjoy a free gift provided by the employer.

Rewards and recognition can be fun and create smiles when the workload becomes demanding. Recognition shows that employees are valued, especially if they use their skills and energy for the betterment of the organization. Rewards and recognition tell employees what the organization considers to be important.

Rewards and recognition are, therefore, both *initiators* and *directors* of behavior. They provide incentives to repeat good work. They provide a guide as to what is considered excellent work. Although contributions to organizational success must ultimately be initiated personally by the employees themselves, external rewards can encourage and inspire employees to excel at their jobs.

3. WHAT DO EMPLOYEES APPRECATE?

A number of studies, formal and informal, have attempted to ascertain what employees appreciate at work. What cultivates a sense of comfort on the job so that employees can successfully contribute to the organization? What influences employees to consistently produce, as well as to tackle new tasks?

Employees consistently indicate that their work is more meaningful and productive if they understand how they are contributing, and are part of the decision-making that affects their work. They value open communication, interesting challenges, and camaraderie. They also appreciate personal attention, feedback, and praise. They become motivated (or maintain their motivation) when their efforts are acknowledged. *They appreciate appreciation!*

Rewards and recognition are a means of demonstrating appreciation. Employees indicate that recognition is most satisfying when carried out by a known and respected supervisor, in front of coworkers, and during a special time set aside for the purpose of recognition.

If a *reward* is given, employees indicate that they appreciate the fact that organizations will bother to go to the expense of purchasing gifts, prizes, and other monetary awards. At the same time, organizations should make sure that the expense makes sense. Organizations should select rewards that are:

- needed or wanted by employees (instead of something that will never be used)
- useful (for fun, career advancement, or making life easier)
- something that employees would not normally do for themselves
- tied to the accomplishment (perhaps even visible to customers or the community)
- something that will be cherished, or at least a positive reminder of the recognition
- in sync with the diversity and lifestyle of the employees.

For example, employees who work two jobs just to put food on the dinner table may not be interested in a gift certificate to an expensive golf course. In fact, they may resent the lack of understanding of their lifestyle. However, if a special treat (such as a day of golf) would be welcomed, then the reward may be appropriate. It should be evident that there was thought behind the selection of the reward.

Successful managers realize that employees can respond to recognition by becoming motivated, productive, and loyal to the organization. These leaders also know that rewards and recognition have to be genuine and valued by employees. Employees want to be rewarded for:

- consistently hard work (not just for working "above and beyond the call of duty")
- seeing a project through to the end (especially if the project involved a difficult collaboration)

- being instrumental in solving a problem (whether for the short term or long term)
- surviving a stressful time period (such as audits, crises, major changes)
- developing knowledge and leadership.

Most employees do not want to "look a gift horse in the mouth." They appreciate the intention of organizations to recognize employees. However, they also may question the expense if they see money "wasted" on trivial rewards that are meaningless.

Managers may find it difficult to dispense rewards and recognition when they are acutely aware of employee weaknesses and of other areas in the organization that could use financial support. They may not understand why employees cannot just do their jobs as expected, and then, *on their own*, take the initiative to do more.

No organization should depend strictly on rewards and recognition for motivating employees to do their jobs. They should not feel the need to dangle incentives every time they want employees to work a little harder. If supervisors are providing training, coaching, resources, and positive reinforcement, the rewards and recognition should be the icing on the cake. Employees will benefit, as will the organization.

4. WHAT ARE EXAMPLES OF REWARDS AND RECOGNITION?

There are hundreds of suggestions about how employees can be rewarded. Catalogs, websites, and business publications are dedicated to information about prizes, plaques, equipment, tools, certificates, and so forth. Reward and recognition committees often brainstorm about what can be purchased that is appropriate, useful, and complimentary.

It is crucial to remember that cost-free recognition often has as much impact as monetary rewards. Organizations do not have to spend money to provide praise.

Employees remember when their work has been acknowledged, even if positive reinforcement occurs often. Can anyone be complimented too many times? If rewards are simply not affordable, then spend *time*, spend *effort*, spend *sincerity*, and spend *thoughtfulness* on recognizing employees.

It is also important to keep in mind that work and fun do not have to be completely separate concepts. If humor and camaraderie are encouraged, it does not mean that employees are so busy having a good time that they are unproductive. Organizations that include short-term activities and events that encourage people to interact, socialize, laugh, and share support and recognition are going to see increased productivity. If employees are comfortable and relaxed, they treat customers better, work together more effectively, and strive to support the work of the organization. Short breaks that give employees a chance to relax and connect can be a very effective form of low-cost recognition.

The following are just a fraction of reward and recognition ideas. All of the suggestions are designed to encourage employees to "keep up the good work" and feel proud of their contributions to the organization.

Informal Rewards And Recognition

- "catch" employees doing something *right*
- thank- you note (personal or posted) from a senior manager
- small certificate to cover lunch, pizza, movies, books
- positive letters from customers disseminated and posted
- photographs of successes posted
- quick announcement about employee success at a routine meeting (included in the minutes)
- phone call after a difficult event (e.g., long meeting, presentation, customer confrontation)
- "WANTED" posters with information about excellent employees to look for and compliment
- small, humorous or meaningful gift (a unique paperweight, thank you ribbon, buttons, hats)
- food (keeping in mind special dietary concerns)
- surprise thank-you visit, candy on a desk, message in a mailbox
- coupons handed out as compliments, accumulated for catalog prizes
- standing ovation when entering a meeting or in front of customers.

Tailored Rewards And Recognition

- team of the week (flowers, photos, descriptions of tasks) posted for customers and coworkers
- camera to photograph success stories
- special pin to signify years of service or special contributions
- employee time with senior management (lunch, personal meeting)
- invitation to senior management and board meetings for a personal thank-you
- newsletter recognition section
- trophy, plaque, jacket
- invitation to represent staff at senior management planning sessions
- cafeteria menus or events named after an employee
- quality award–or customer service award
- "mystery shopper" identifying excellent service and rewarding "on the spot"

Stress-Reducing Rewards And Recognition

- certificates to bowling, sporting events, concerts, restaurants, theme parks, tours, etc.
- compensatory ("comp") time
- book club or books-on-tape/CD selections
- establishment of on-site dry cleaners, exercise equipment, take-out foods
- special events such as Safety Picnic, holiday gift baskets, early dismissal
- "Oscars" and "Emmys" for specific accomplishments
- closer parking space
- special clothing labeled with organizational logos, such as sneakers, socks, visors, bandannas
- prizes for "Give Your Boss a Prize"

Educational Rewards And Recognition

- conference attendance, with travel, representing the organization
- special training opportunities

- seminars on topics related to personal life, such as raising teenagers, buying a car, paying for college, etc.
- visits to similar businesses, representing the organization
- tours of plants, vendor headquarters, similar organizations
- promotional information about employee education, training, special hobbies (with permission, of course)

The suggestions above are designed to take note of employee accomplishments. They can build morale and loyalty to the organization.

Employees also develop pride and loyalty if they can depend upon their leaders to create a strong public image of the organization. Positive publicity, advertisements, awards, and community involvement can build the reputation of the organization. Employees gain recognition when they are able to *proudly* answer the question "Where do you work? "

5. SHOULD MANAGERS BE RECOGNIZED?

The guidelines for recognizing managers are slightly different than for employees. Although it is important to pay attention to the accomplishments of organizational leaders, there is generally the perception among employees and colleagues that managers are already being paid to go the extra mile, and are expected to be role modeling exceptional work behaviors.

But managers, too, need motivation. They deserve recognition for achieving particularly difficult tasks and for making significant contributions to the organization. The type of recognition may be different than for frontline employees, but the meaning is very similar. The rewards and recognition that are most appreciated by managers build their career and reputation and give employees faith in leadership. Recognition can provide details on the work activities of leaders, defining how they spend their time advocating for the employees and the organization.

Rewards such as luncheons, certificates, training, and other recognition are appropriate for both employees and managers. In addition, managers should receive recognition that will be respected by their peers, such as public acknowledgment, title changes, plaques that can be displayed, promotions, and monetary rewards.

6. CAN THE RECOGNITION PROCESS BE FAIR?

The rewards and recognition process can be terribly unfair if implemented improperly. Barriers to fairness include:

Favoritism

When individuals are recognized because they make a point of calling attention to themselves, or because they steal the credit, the recognition process can feel pointless. If friends, "stars," or more visible employees are always rewarded (thereby ignoring those who are working behind the scenes or without benefit of special relationships), the process becomes resented. Clear criteria for selection can eliminate this barrier.

Ignoring The Team

Many team members feel strongly that if a team accomplishes an important task, recognition should go to the entire team, regardless of the level of individual contributions. If the team members themselves are asked to select a fellow team member to be recognized, they may want to make it clear that it took the work of all members of the team, and all should be recognized. Or they may quickly reach consensus and identify the one team member who contributed the most by taking the lead, or solving a problem.

Circumstances will dictate whether the entire team should be recognized, or whether an individual should be singled out. If the team is not consulted on the process, or clear criteria have not been previously established, teamwork can become eroded by an unfair process.

Blinders

Rewards and recognition can only occur if supervisors pay attention. If the accomplishments of employees are not even noticed, then formal recognition cannot occur. This barrier can be particularly annoying to employees who see coworkers from other departments receiving recognition (formally and informally), when their own supervisor is oblivious or uncaring. If reward and recognition systems are in place, supervisors who are responsible for distributing them should be aware of:

- the reward and recognition system
- the purpose and benefits of rewards and recognition
- the criteria for selection
- the types of rewards available
- the possible impact of the choice of recipients
- the need for fairness.

Discouragement

Occasionally, employees may feel discouraged because they did *not* receive recognition. For example, if employees have achieved an important goal and then see other coworkers rewarded for a similar or lesser accomplishment, the value of the recognition process can decline. Employees begin to ask: Why should we bother to go the extra mile if our efforts will go unnoticed and others will receive recognition?

This barrier is tied to the question of the purpose of rewards and recognition. Before providing visible rewards and recognition, it is essential that supervisors be well versed on the *purpose* of the recognition and the criteria for selection. Supervisors should ask themselves when considering whether to publicly recognize an employee:

- Will the recipient be proud?
- Will colleagues also be proud?
- Will some be resentful because they carried out the same tasks successfully?
- Is there a way to clarify why the recognition choice was made? (There will still be some grumblers, but coworkers will at least know the reasons for a decision and will probably begrudgingly acknowledge that the choice was fair.)
- Is there a better way to share the recognition, or change the focus of the recognition? (For example, rather than rewards for just a

few, pizza is provided for everyone who participated on a project, with a special public thanks for outstanding participants.)

Timing

The timing of recognition can often determine the response of the recipient. Supervisors should consider:

- The middle of a project may be more appropriate than the end, to keep spirits and motivation high.
- Public acknowledgment may embarrass some employees, or cause them to be victims of uncomfortable teasing by those who resent hard workers. On the other hand, private acknowledgment that is *not* witnessed by coworkers, may take the excitement and pride away from the experience. Consider the *employee* and the *working conditions* when determining the timing.
- Recognition is often welcomed by employees when it is conducted during a much-needed break, during a particularly stressful period, or at the beginning of a significant change.
- Rewards and recognition that are established on a routine basis such as monthly or quarterly should be provided as promised. Many employees will work hard to earn a monthly safety award, or they will look forward to the quarterly staff meeting when accomplishments are announced. If scheduled, meet the time frame.
- Surprise rewards and recognition are often a needed boost for employees, regardless of the working conditions or stress levels. Employees can be informally "caught" doing excellent work at any time.

Rewards and recognition are based on the philosophy that employees who are openly appreciated will willingly provide better productivity, customer service, and other positive work behaviors. If employees feel that every effort was made by the organization to carry out rewards and recognition in a fair manner, they will develop motivation and loyalty.

7. WHAT IF REWARDS ARE NOT AFFORDABLE?

Rewards and recognition do not have to be major budgetary expenses to be successful. It is fun and exciting to receive tangible rewards, and employees will probably express their appreciation for receiving a gift, a plaque, or a luncheon.

But what employees really want is their work to be noticed. The best recognition is the spontaneous praise from a boss, the personal thank you from the chief executive officer, or the public announcement of the accomplishments of a team. The goal is to boost pride in work and cultivate employee effort and loyalty. Free compliments, if delivered with sincerity by a leader who truly has been paying attention, are affordable and a very powerful motivator. Free recognition can produce high employee satisfaction and productivity.

8. WHAT ARE THE STEPS TO IMPLEMENTING REWARDS AND RECOGNITION?

When a formal reward and recognition process is established by an organization, the following steps to implementation are suggested:

Gather And Research

Search the bookshelves and the Internet for ideas about tangible and intangible rewards. Consult with other organizations, whether or not they are similar, gathering ideas and suggestions.

Observe

Observe existing forms of rewards and recognition in the organization, even if not formalized. What do supervisors do already? What is posted, announced, printed in newsletters? Are there plaques, trophies, and certificates on display?

Evaluate

Evaluate formal systems that have been established in the past. Are they institutionalized, routine, and still appreciated? Were they abandoned? Why? Are they well known and utilized? Underutilized?

Team Up

Team up a committee of supervisors and employees to discuss the *purpose* of rewards and recognition. Why should a system exist? What is the *goal*? Avoid discussing specific details at first. Concentrate on *why* the reward and recognition system is being established.

With the committee, make a long list of what work activities they think should be formally recognized. List categories such as projects, service, safety, and individual accomplishments (e.g., certification, training) that the committee feels should get special attention. Then begin to prioritize the activities that everyone agrees should be recognized. It is not necessary to create a reward for everything on the list. Start out with a short list of areas where rewards and recognition can be implemented. Make sure that the reasons for the selections are clear.

Brainstorm

Then brainstorm a separate wish list consisting of three columns headed "FREE," "AFFORDABLE," and "EXPENSIVE."

Some committees prefer to know budget limitations in advance, while others would rather brainstorm without restrictions. Either way, the committee should concentrate on two questions:

1. What would the employees of this organization *appreciate*?
2. What is an *appropriate* reward or recognition?

For example, in the AFFORDABLE column, the committee may put "Doughnuts every Friday morning." A treat on Friday mornings may be appropriate because Fridays are especially busy and employees may need a thank-you for a tough week, and a boost to get through a challenging day. Once it is established that a reward on Friday mornings would be a good motivator, it may be pointed out that the employees are frequently discussing health and weight concerns, and doughnuts (although enjoyed) may not necessarily be *appreciated*. If it has been clarified *why* a recognition would be motivational on Friday mornings, then connect the *why* to an appropriate reward.

This exercise will certainly take time, as participants debate the suggestions and consider the barriers to fairness in implementing rewards and recognition. They may not agree on what employees will appreciate, but they are not expected to reach consensus. This process is crucial in identifying the concerns and impressions of the committee. Important information will emerge. It becomes easier to reach consensus later.

After brainstorming, even if not finished, discuss the key points that seemed to emerge from the discussion. Are the likes and dislikes of employees apparent? Are the reasons for recognition clear? Are strategies for overcoming barriers apparent? Ask:

- Does it appear that employees would respond more positively to several small recognition strategies or one big one?
- Can any of the FREE and AFFORDABLE activities be implemented immediately by managers who wish to get started in their own departments?
- Should any of the FREE activities be listed as immediate expectations for everyone? (Examples might be free praise, thank-you notes, etc.)
- Which of the ideas are most appealing to the committee?

At this point, the budget may need to be introduced as a deciding factor. Depending upon the organization, the final selection of the *type* of rewards and recognition should be determined either by the committee or by the leadership of the organization. Matching the reward to expenses can get tricky, especially because the expense will need justification. Make sure that the purpose of the recognition is clear.

Establish Criteria

Establish the *criteria* for selecting a recipient of rewards and recognition, including *why* the reward is being disseminated. The criteria not only help in the final selection process, but provide a justification for the expense.

For example, it may be determined that every month a different team should be recognized. In discussing the purpose of the recognition, the committee may decide that the ability of the team to work together to solve a problem should be emphasized because teamwork is a core value of the organization and problem-solving contributes to productivity and cost-effectiveness. Emphasis would not be on the *product* of a team, or the *safety* of a team, but the *process in which the team worked together to solve a problem.* The criteria for selection may include:

The Team:

• discussed the problem as a group, involving all team members in identifying and analyzing the problem

• listened to ideas and suggestions, and consulted outside the team

• utilized unique skills of team members

• resolved differences in order to solve the problem

• conducted research, including pilots and testing, to become well informed about the problem

• reached consensus about how to solve the problem.

Notice that the criteria do not include "SOLVED THE PROBLEM" because the purpose of the rewards and recognition was to acknowledge the teamwork *process.*

• For each set of criteria, determine the *nomination/identification* process and how *proof* will be gathered. Who will know if the criteria were actually fulfilled? Should observation and selection be up to the supervisors? Can employees/teams nominate themselves and coworkers? What evidence needs to be provided? Clarify exactly who selects, what steps they take, and how rewards will be disseminated.

• For each set of criteria, consider the possible negative fallout. Once a reward is given, will it make sense to all employees why the reward was given to the person or team selected?

• Create a timeline for implementing the reward and recognition process, including:

  • phased-in implementation
  • education of employees and supervisors prior to implementation
  • opportunities for feedback *before* and *after* the first reward has been disseminated.

The committee responsible for rewards and recognition should meet routinely to monitor the implementation of the system and the impact of the process. There will definitely be modifications as supervisors and employees become comfortable with formalizing a system. Above all, the committee should keep educating about the *purpose* of rewards and recognition in the first place.

9. WHAT IF AN ORGANIZATION IS STRUGGLING?

When organizations are struggling with financial cutbacks, layoffs, and other changes that can affect employee morale, it is crucial that recognition continue to take place. Employees will need to maintain productivity, even while they are concerned about job security. They will need to feel appreciated at times when organizational leadership may appear to be insensitive or distracted. They will need the motivation to use their skills so that they can continue to contribute and to build qualifications.

In times of organizational stress, the process of rewards and recognition may seem like an extraneous task that is not nearly as important as survival on the job, or success of an organization. But it is in times of stress that organizations will benefit from recognizing employees. A thank-you, public acknowledgment, or personal note will not only demonstrate employee support during difficult times, but will encourage employees to concentrate on the work that is still necessary to accomplish.

10. HOW DO YOU MEASURE THE IMPACT OF REWARDS AND RECOGNITION?

The effectiveness of the recognition program is first measured in terms of the *value* of the recognition to the employees. It is of no value if they do not care about it or do not take it seriously. If valued, rewards and recognition can directly reinforce desired behavior or performance.

The organization may already measure the quality of work with performance appraisals, 360 assessments, employee surveys, and so forth.

Measurement of rewards and recognition requires quantitative and qualitative documentation and verification of:

- increased productivity
- reduced redundancy and duplication of effort
- unusual innovations, especially if they were replicated elsewhere or saved time and money
- increased efficiency, especially if it is permanent, and resulted in savings or new revenue sources
- superior accomplishments, with the organization gaining from a new product, new expertise, or new systems.

These forms of documentation may be anecdotal, with tracking records and data accumulated over time, such as staff turnover and transfer requests. But they still provide a useful picture in assessing changes as a result of implementing rewards and recognition.

Organizations can also look at the comfort level of employees, and job satisfaction through employee surveys, focus groups, and team conferences. If employees feel comfortable and appreciated at work, they will produce, and will desire to stay with an organization that treats them well.

After implementing a reward and recognition system, compare employee turnover figures and longevity of employees with the distribution of recognition and rewards throughout the organization. Check to see if the organization is not recognizing employees who have been productive and loyal. Make sure that employees have a record of their rewards and recognition in their personnel file, or in the form of a certificate, newsletter, or personal note.

INDEX